I ♥ Shania Twain

# I ♥ Shania Twain

## A Celebration of the Queen of Country Pop

COURTNEY SHEA

RUNNING PRESS
PHILADELPHIA

Running Press
Hachette Book Group
1290 Avenue of the Americas, New York, NY 10104
www.runningpress.com
@Running_Press

First Edition: August 2025

Published by Running Press, an imprint of Hachette Book Group, Inc. The Running Press name and logo are trademarks of Hachette Book Group, Inc.



Illustrations by Helen Green
Cover photo by George Holz Photography
Print book cover and interior design by Justine Kelley

Library of Congress Control Number: 2025933405

ISBNs: 979-8-89414-022-3 (hardcover), 979-8-89414-023-0 (ebook)

Printed in China

1010

10 9 8 7 6 5 4 3 2 1

# CONTENTS

INTRODUCTION

# WHY I ❤ Shania

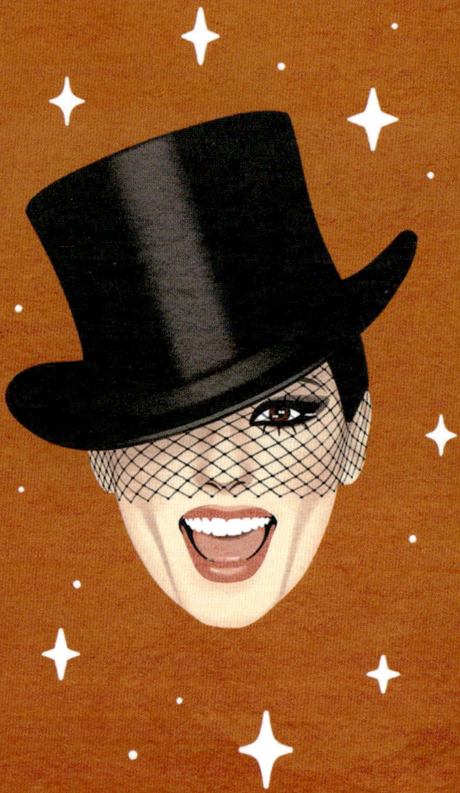

In 2024 Shania Twain was tapped to fill the lauded "legend" slot at the Glastonbury Music Festival—that annual spectacle of music's cool kids in fashion-forward rain gear, situated in the English countryside. Before the performance, she had joked with the media that she wanted to arrive on horseback—a not entirely surprising objective, given the number of times she has involved her beloved equines in her act. And a not entirely unfulfilled one, either: When Shania did take the Glastonbury stage, it was behind a curtain of drag queens and dancers riding hobby horses that eventually parted to reveal the legend of the day, dressed hat-to-toe in powder pink ruffles. It was the kind of wink that Shania has been sharing with her fans for as long as she has been performing: playful, always, but not without a sense of purpose—a commitment to inclusivity and positivity that is as quintessentially Shania as leopard print.

The summer music festival circuit has been a key aspect of the recent "Shaniassance," an era of enhanced appreciation that kicked off in 2020 when Shania released her fifth studio album, *The Queen of Me*, just as Gen Z was familiarizing itself with her back catalog and country music was taking over the mainstream. In 2022 she showed up onstage during Harry Styles's set at Coachella. Taylor Swift may be the contemporary template for a crossover icon, but just ask Taylor who charted her course (or watch the TikTok Swift posted, paying homage to "Mother"). It's tempting to say Shania walked so Taylor could run, only Shania Twain never walked anywhere. She stomped and shimmied and line-danced and horseback-rode her way to the top.

It was a couple of months into the writing process of this book that I got a chance to speak with my subject directly. When we connected over the phone, I could hear wind whipping in the background. Turns out Shania was taking my call from the saddle, helping a friend to herd their cattle on a ranch in Alberta, Canada. (*Of course she was!*) As a journalist, I have chatted with celebrities from their private jets and holiday homes and most often from their publicist's office, but speaking to someone mid-cattle wrangle was a first for me. And a pretty great reason to heart Shania, come to think of it. (Spoiler alert: There are many.)

See also: Her ability to keep reinventing herself and surprising her fans after decades in the spotlight; her commitment to lifting up other artists and bringing progressive values to country music; the way she has taken so much personal adversity and channeled it into a musical catalog that could get the Grinch out onto the dance floor. It is almost impossible to pick just one favorite from Shania's ample canon of dance jams, barn burners, and unabashedly schmaltzy classics that have provided the soundtrack to our lives (and our shower singing sessions). Shania's hits have broken conventions and broken records. "From This Moment On" is still a mainstay of wedding ceremonies, twenty-five years later. In 2022 *Billboard* tapped 1998's "Man! I Feel Like a Woman!" as the greatest karaoke song of all time, and I'm certainly

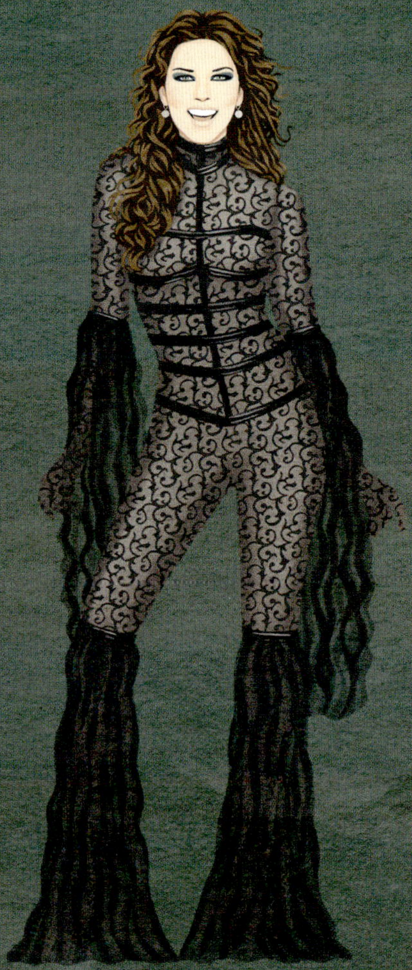

not going to argue the point. For me, though, the Shania track that resonates most is the first single on her 2002 album *Up!*, "I'm Gonna Getcha Good!" Maybe because it best describes my own Shania journey . . .

I was an angsty teen when she was first climbing the charts, caught under the flannel and apathy-draped influence of bands like Nirvana and Pearl Jam. Being Canadian, it was impossible not to be aware of the powder keg of talent that had erupted out of Timmins, Ontario, and was selling more records than all the grunge gods put together. But country? That was for old people. And "new country"—the modern, pop-infused anthems that were reinventing the genre—that was just far too sunny for my Gen X sensibility. I wasn't ready yet, but Shania was undeterred. "*I'm gonna getcha while I've got you in sight . . .*"

I entered college around the same time that Shania entered the global icon stage of her career. She was charting in Australia and Germany as I was still resisting—dancing to Destiny's Child and Eminem at parties and listening to Lauryn Hill and Fiona Apple in my dorm room, developing a feminist worldview that did not, as of yet, include a certain crop-topped icon. I had a lot to learn, but Shania didn't break stride. "*I'm gonna getcha if it takes all night . . .*"

I can still remember the night everything changed. It was a friend's birthday bash: Everyone was standing around the dark bar, sipping and chatting and then suddenly—"ba-bah-na-nah, na-na-nah," went the unmistakable opening riff of "Man! I Feel Like a Woman!" "Let's go, girls," Shania commanded, and every last girl and boy and pulsating human being in the vicinity obeyed. There I was, putting my spin on the song's burlesque-inspired dance moves, singing along to every last word—these lyrics that had apparently implanted themselves in my subconscious. Not just that Shania hit, but all of them. The DJ knew a rapt audience when he saw one, and the rest of the night turned into an unofficial tribute concert.

"*Like I should, I'll get you good,*" Shania promised. And she did.

At time of this writing it's a decade later and I have come to appreciate not just her music but her commitment to issues that matter and her refusal to bow to the haters. (Because she's going to wear a crop top whenever she darn well pleases.) These are *my* reasons to heart Shania. For a good friend of mine, it was seeing her live in Vegas (twice!). For the woman I spotted wearing a COME ON OVER concert tee on the subway, it's the way she has maintained her optimism amid so much personal adversity. Shania's appeal is as broad as a wide-brim Stetson, and a whole new generation of country fans have been discovering her excellence. There are a lot of so-called "heritage acts" cashing in on their legend status these days, but few of them are still attracting new audiences the way Shania is. Even fewer can take credit for a modern music landscape where everyone from Beyoncé to Lana Del Rey to Post Malone is going country, riding on the ruffled, sequined, leopard-printed coattails of the original and eternal Queen of Country Pop.

Now feels like a great time to look back on her extraordinary career and life: For inspiration, for insight, to revisit the memorable moments and list the many reasons to love Shania. Some might surprise you (did you know she wrote her first song at ten years old?); others will spill the sweet tea (the real story behind the Brad Pitt reference). Of course, we will pay homage to the most memorable fashion statements and explore the origins of the Shaniassance while we're at it. The reasons to heart this woman are endless so let's giddy up and get to it.

CHAPTER ONE

# Because Girlfriend Was Born as Far Away from Superstardom as You Can Get

“From this moment, I have been blessed . . .”

Shania Twain didn't grow up anywhere near Nashville or Hollywood, but thousands of miles from the bright lights, deep in the Canadian backwoods. She didn't even grow up Shania Twain. Eilleen Regina Edwards arrived in the world on August 28, 1965—named after her two grandmothers, the middle kid between an older sister, Jill, and a younger sister, Carrie Ann. By the time she turned two, her parents had split and her mother, Sharon, moved the family to Timmins, Ontario, a mining town that was then famous for its goldfields, and is now famous for Shania fricking

Twain. Her last name came from her mom's second husband, Jerry Twain, a forest worker and member of the First Nations Ojibwa Tribe who adopted Eilleen and her sisters. Next came a baby brother, Darryl, and then another brother when the family adopted Jerry's nephew, Mark. The "Twain Gang," as they were known, comprised five kids from four dads and two moms, but they didn't use terms like *half-siblings* or *stepdad*. They were just one big family, although not always a happy one.

In the Twain household, domestic violence was an ongoing issue between Jerry and Sharon, who also suffered from debilitating depression. Money was a constant source of stress, and when the electric bill didn't get paid, the kids would go to bed freezing. Little Eilleen daydreamed about the families who ate roast beef while she often had to make due with mustard sandwiches, but even in the hardest times, there was always music: Her parents played classic country in the house and they listened to the hits on the car radio, with Eilleen always picking up the harmony. Her mom took notice and pretty much any

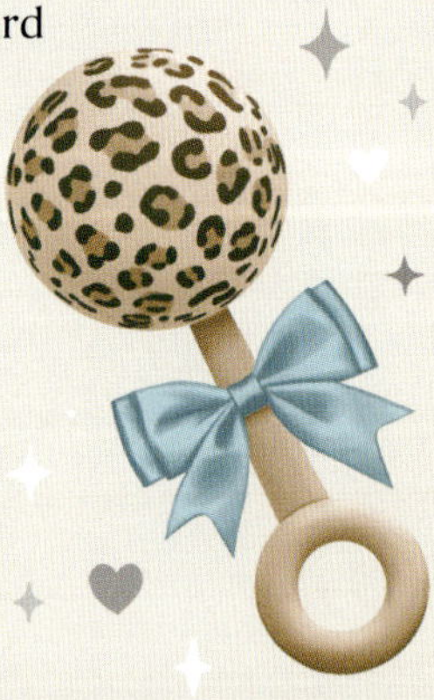

**BECAUSE SHE IS A PROUD MEMBER OF THE TEMAGAMI FIRST NATION, OWING TO HER ADOPTED FATHER'S INDIGENOUS HERITAGE.**

As a kid, she spent summers at the Mattagami reserve with her grandparents, learning to hunt, chip wood, and snare rabbits. She has always taken pride in her connection to Canada's First Nations people. In 2021, she narrated *For Love*, a documentary about the overrepresentation of Indigenous children in the foster system.

time they were in public she would push her daughter to sing—plopping her up on a jukebox at the local diner to make sure the audience could see her. By eight years old, Eilleen could play guitar—her natural ability was obvious and her mother's ambition was unrelenting. It was illegal for a kid to sing in a bar while they were serving alcohol, so the future superstar would take the stage after last call (1 a.m.), performing standards for the late-night revelers who were still finishing their beers. It was an exhausting existence, but even then Eilleen sensed that singing would be her way out.

A lot of her friends played with Barbies, but dolls cost money, so Eilleen played with grass, giving the different blades their own names and personalities, creating

**BECAUSE SHE ALWAYS DREAMED BIG.**

Other top childhood fantasies included being a backup singer for Stevie Wonder and getting kidnapped by Frank Sinatra (because she would feel too guilty abandoning her family, but if she got taken . . .).

**BECAUSE SHE WROTE HER FIRST SONG—A BALLAD CALLED "MAMA WON'T YOU COME OUT TO PLAY"—AT TEN YEARS OLD.**

By that time, Sharon Twain was suffering from depression, spending days at a time in bed, and her daughter hoped the song might inspire her to feel better.

a make-believe world that inspired her earliest efforts at songwriting. She loved the creative freedom and the opportunity for self-expression, but the limelight—not so much. In her grade school band, she played trombone and once got so nervous during a live performance that she actually peed her pants (covering up the embarrassing incident with a glass of water).

Away from school she booked her first TV gig on *The Tommy Hunter Show*, singing Willie Nelson's classic "Blue Eyes Crying in the Rain." Country was the music of her childhood: Willie, Waylon, Tanya Tucker, and her idol Dolly Parton (another girl from the backwoods whose talent took her all the way to the top). But teenage Eilleen

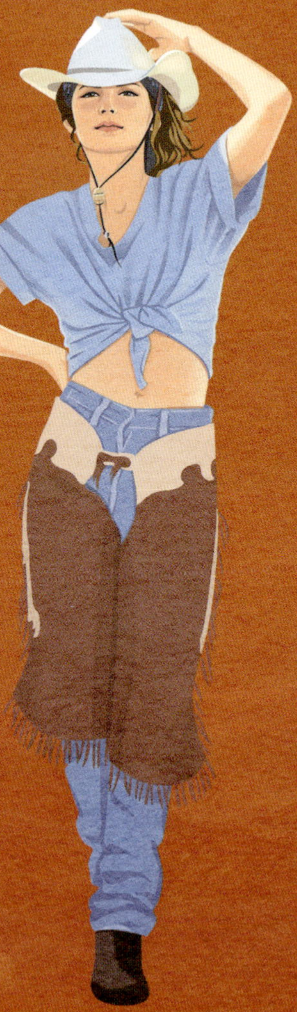

## BECAUSE SHE LOVES DOLLY PARTON.

So many of today's pop and country superstars credit Shania with being the first, but, for the girl from Timmins, there was another legend from the backwoods lighting a path. Dolly's "Coat of Many Colors" was one of the first songs little Eilleen Twain learned to play on guitar. Later she and Dolly got a chance to play the song together on *The Oprah Winfrey Show*. "She's her own world . . . Dolly's every little girl's perfect example of what is possible when you come from nothing," Shania says.

was more interested in rocking out than strumming another sob story. She loved the energy of pop music and also the look—teased hair, spandex, leg warmers.

By the time she finished high school in 1983, she was singing in a cover band called Flirt—she missed her graduation because she was on tour. (She even gave her prom dress to a friend.) That same year, she moved to Toronto, a big city to match her big dreams. In the winters, she would book as many bar gigs as she could manage, but the pay wasn't enough to live on. Every summer

**BECAUSE THE DIVA HAD TO START SOMEWHERE.**

When Shania first started singing at Deerhurst—six nights a week onstage plus extra performances in the piano bar—she had never worn high heels or heavy makeup. She looks back on this time as an invaluable master class in what it takes to create not just great music, but a great show. (Hint: There's no such thing as too many sequins.)

she would go home to Timmins to earn money planting trees, always working on her music and recording demos on the side.

Everything seemed to be heading in the right direction until November 1, 1987. She was in Toronto when she got the phone call that would change her life forever. Her parents had been in a car accident—both of them killed instantly. Her grief was tremendous, but so was her sense of responsibility. With three younger siblings still in school and no one to care for them, Eilleen moved back to Timmins, planning to give up her musical ambitions and "get a real job," but fate (that is, a friend of the family who worked in the music business) intervened.

Deerhurst Resort was a cottage country getaway—sort of like the place in *Dirty Dancing*—where guests were treated to a glitzy review show called Viva Vegas. Eilleen got a job performing radio hits and Broadway classics—not exactly her style, but, hey, it was music and the pay was enough to support her family. She spent three years singing and dancing, mastering the quick-change and wearing her body weight in sequins, until one night when an entertainment lawyer from Nashville came to see the act. He knew somebody who knew another somebody, and by 1991 the future

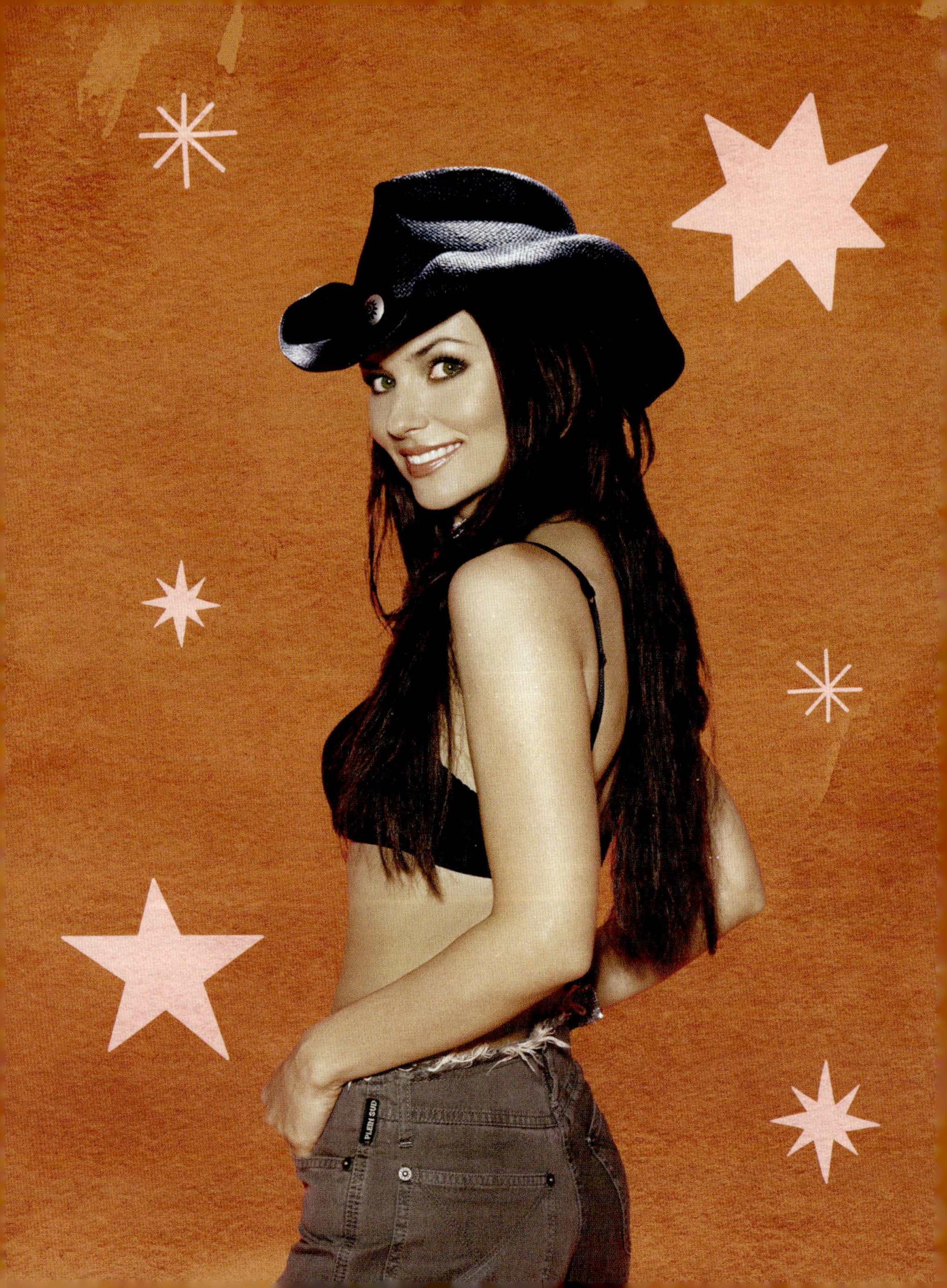

**BECAUSE SHE WAS NEVER AFRAID OF A LITTLE HARD WORK.**

While dreaming of a career in the music business, Shania had several non-glam side hustles: tree planter as well as sales associate, house cleaner, and gigs at two separate McDonald's locations in Toronto where her favorite station was the drive-through and her favorite snack was the fries.

superstar had signed her first record deal with Mercury Records' country division in the United States. It was the big break she had dreamed of, but there was no big paycheck—at least not yet. She couldn't afford to move to Nashville and instead stayed in Timmins, working part time as a department store salesgirl and spending all her free time tucked away in a remote cabin on the shores of Lake Kenogamissi, writing the foundations for many of her future hits. But when she shared her songs with the record label, they weren't convinced it was the right sound for an emerging country artist. Instead, her debut album featured a bunch of tracks written by other

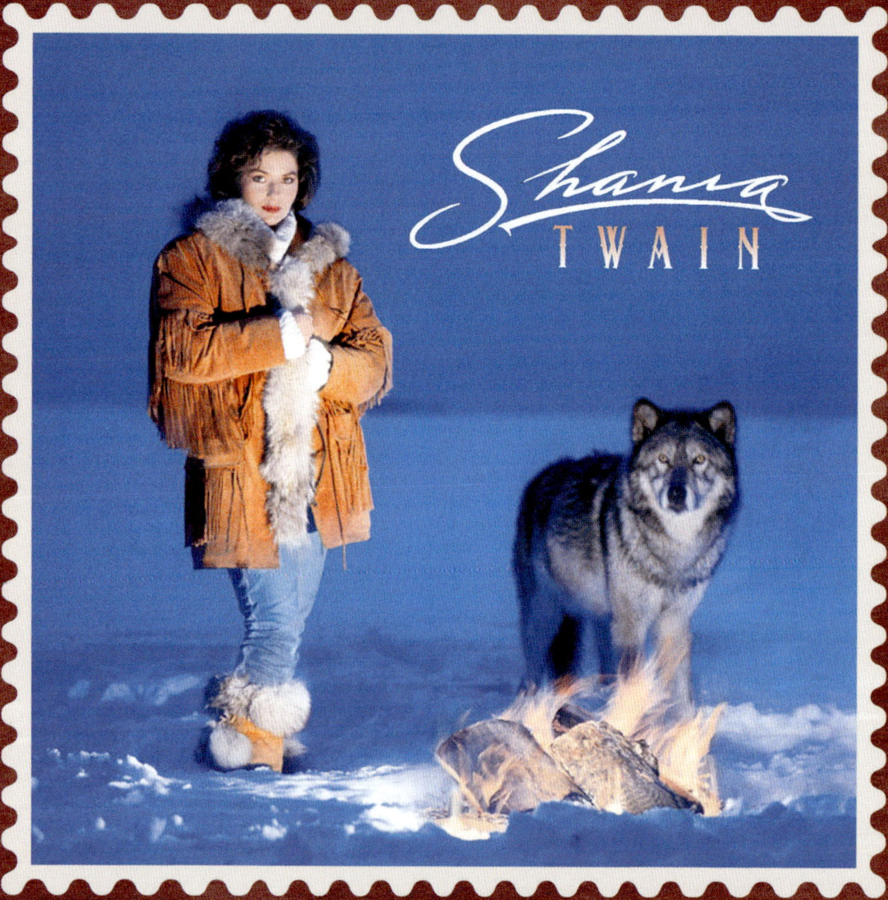
Shania
TWAIN

songwriters, recorded in quick and creatively stifling studio sessions.

The finished product failed to set the world on fire, but it did feature some pretty iconic cover art. And a new name. *Eilleen* didn't exactly scream star power. When it was time to come up with an alternative she thought back to a wardrobe mistress who had worked at Deerhurst, an Ojibwa woman, which felt like a good way to pay tribute to her father's Indigenous heritage. And while she didn't know it then, *Shania* was a prescient choice: The word in Ojibwa means "on my way."

**BECAUSE, YES, THAT'S A REAL WOLF ON HER FIRST ALBUM COVER.**

Real snow, too. The photo shoot happened at a trapper's lodge near her hometown and she arrived by Sno-Cat. "I wanted to keep things close to my roots," Shania has said of the artistic concept—and, just to be sure, she wore authentic mukluks (made by her grandma).

CHAPTER TWO

# Because Nashville Had Never Seen the Likes of Her Before

"That don't impress me much."

The conservative world of country music was not a natural fit for a free-spirited Canadian with a unique sense of humor and a vocabulary full of four-letter words. The Twain family were never churchgoers and etiquette was not a priority as they struggled to put food on the table. Before her first album came out, Shania did media training to polish up this gem and soften her northern accent. But her sense of artistic frustration was harder to dial down: As much as she had wanted the album to sell better, what really killed her was the lack of artistic input she had been given over her first (and maybe her only) shot. But middling sales had an eventual upside, clearing the path for a defining moment of creative expression. Her debut single "What Made You Say That" didn't even crack the top 40, so when it was time to make the music video, the label was largely hands-off, leaving the project (and a minuscule budget) in Shania's hands. Forget high fashion hookups: she bought her wardrobe off the rack at a department store and here's where things get interesting . . .

Hard work, good timing, and a ten-gallon hat's worth of talent are all at the root of Shania's rise to superstardom, but at this particular fork in the road, it all came down to a single piece of clothing: the black crop top that she wears in the "What Made You Say That" video while frolicking in the arms of a nameless paramour. It was not her intention to disrupt the status quo. This was the early nineties, and female celebs like Madonna and Cindy Crawford had turned midriff-baring into a popular cultural norm. But this wasn't pop—it was country, and for the pearl-clutching powers that be, a few inches of exposed female flesh blew the barn doors off. Country Music Television (CMT) actually banned the video from its airwaves for several weeks before finally bowing to public demand.

(Turns out a little scandal isn't the worst thing for a new and unknown artist.)

Meanwhile, European audiences were a lot less prudish. CMT Europe awarded Twain its 1993 Rising Star Award—her first major music accolade. DJs on the other side of the pond didn't have any problem playing the video, and it was on the European airwaves that Shania's talent (and tummy) caught the attention of Mutt Lange, a music producer who would change her life forever.

Lange's reputation was as a rock guy. Then forty-five, he was a major behind-the-scenes power player, producing hit albums for bands like AC/DC, Def Leppard, and Bryan Adams. But he was also into country music—and very into the fresh-faced, midriff-baring brunette from one particular music video. Lange reached out to Shania through her manager. Their first phone call turned into an hours-long creative brainstorming session, where she shared the songs she had been working on and he saw the potential to crank up the twang in a way that had never been done: country music, but bigger, louder, infused with the kind of power production that had turned AC/DC into rock gods. Shania had always seen her music as a pop/country hybrid, and Mutt had the road map for how to make that happen in the studio. Six months after their

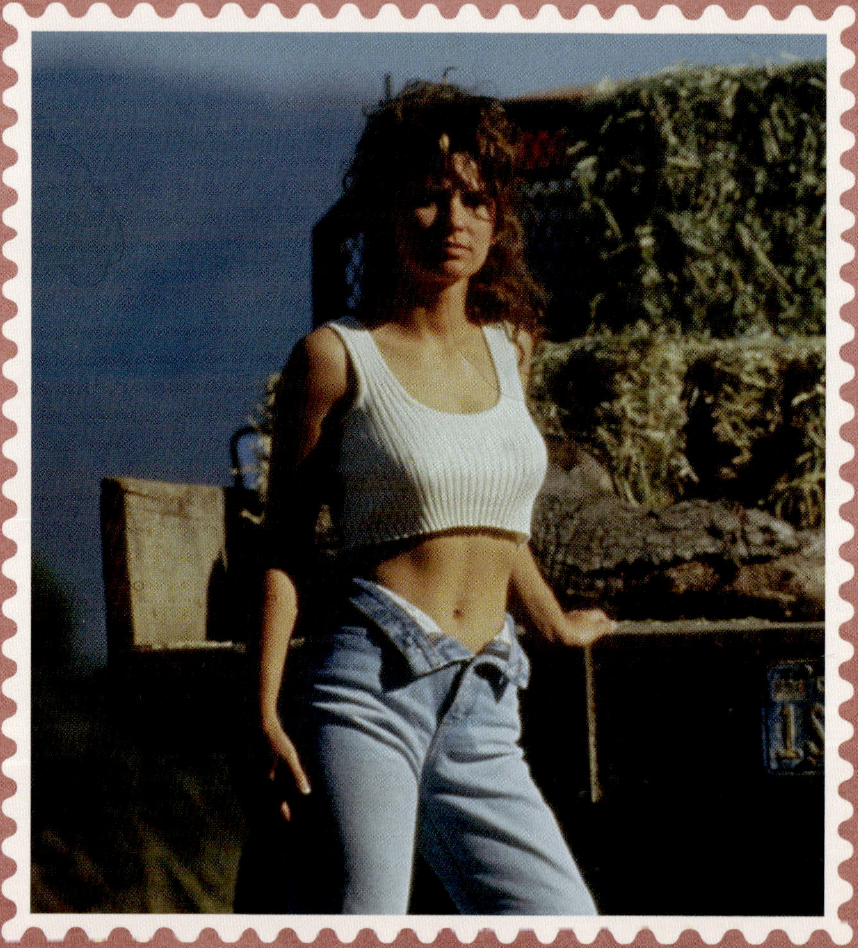

## BECAUSE SHE STILL LOVES THE ODD F-BOMB (EVEN IF PRINCE DIDN'T).

Shania has never been shy about her love of the f-word (and her tendency to use it when the situation dictates). She has also shared the story about how Prince once contacted her about working together. Tragically, the pop legend died before the two got a chance to collaborate, but it might not have worked out anyway. Prince told Shania there was no swearing at his famous Paisley Park estate in Minneapolis, and she wasn't sure if she could abstain for an entire album.

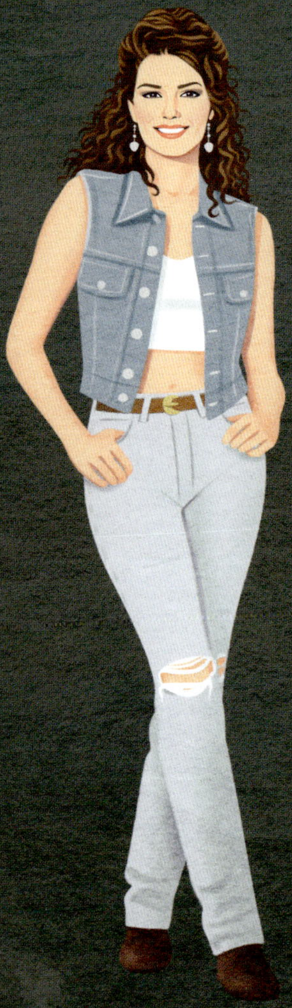

**BECAUSE HOLY HYPOCRISY, BATMAN!**

Never mind that the guy in the video is 100 percent topless, it was Shania's blink-and-you-missed-it belly button that set off a firestorm.

first meeting, they had written a full album's worth of new music, fallen in love, and made it official. For the wedding, they went back to Deerhurst Resort—a full-circle moment and a way to make sure Shania's family could attend. The bride wore a floor-length white cape and the temperature was freezing, even as the fruits of this particular union were about to burn their way up the charts.

It would take some time, though. When *The Woman In Me* came out in 1995, it was just what Shania and Mutt wanted: something totally fresh and original, and the industry gatekeepers reacted accordingly. "Whose Bed Have Your Boots Been Under?" is a cheeky, chart-friendly toe-tapper of a track, where a woman is asking her partner to own up to his infidelity. Both the song itself and the video include all kinds of country iconography from

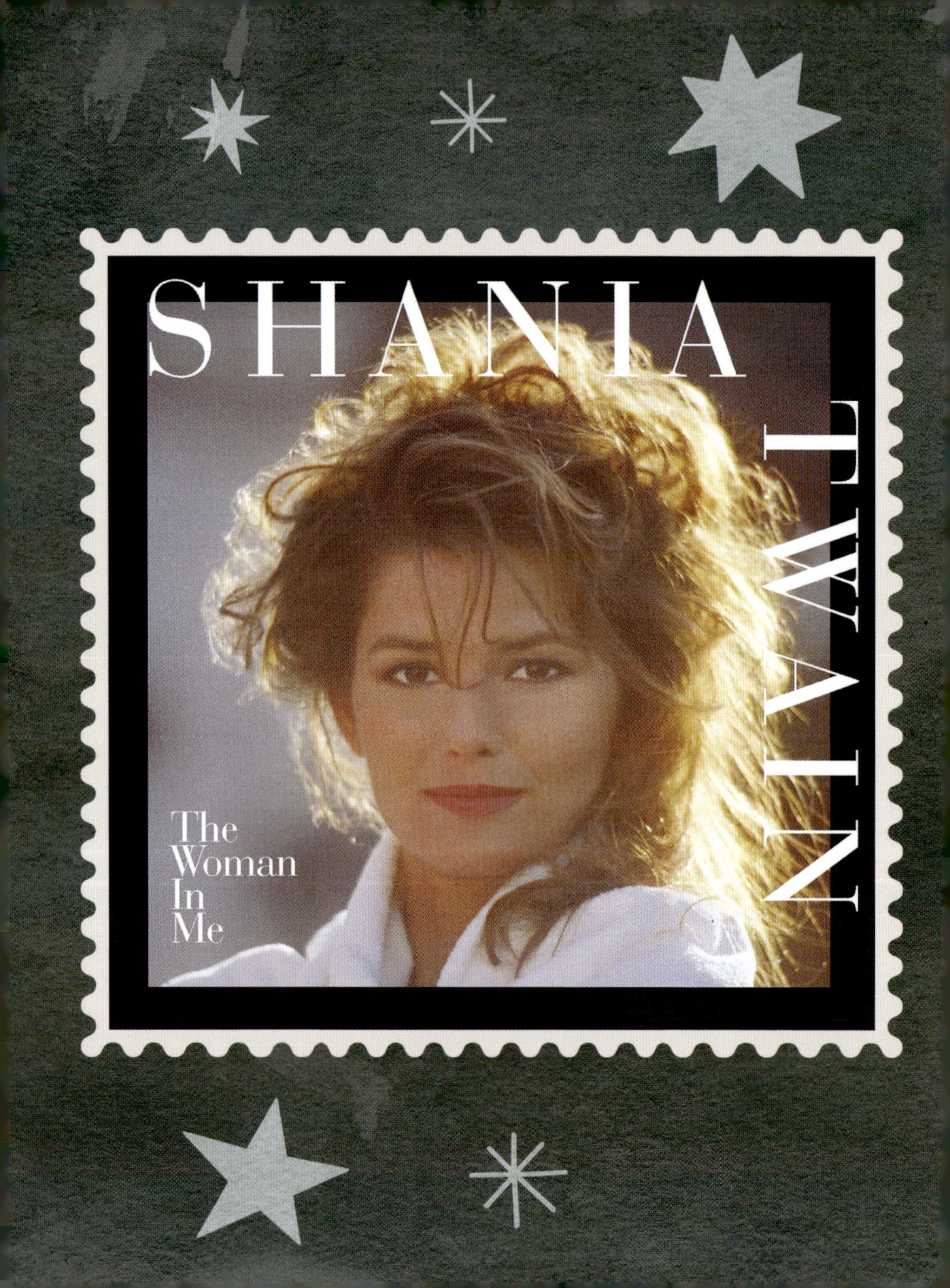
SHANIA
TWAIN
The Woman In Me

**BECAUSE YOU'RE NOBODY UNTIL SOMEBODY BANS YOU.**

Other music legends who have landed on the wrong side of censorship include Duran Duran, Madonna, Twisted Sister, Lady Gaga, and Rihanna—pretty good company.

a pickup truck to a diner full of dudes in Stetsons, but still it wasn't country enough, according to some radio stations that played a role in stalling the album's success. But only for so long. Five months in, "Boots" broke the top 20 on the *Billboard* Country Chart, propelled not by DJs but by public demand.

A month later, "Any Man of Mine" was released and it was all systems firing. The song and the entire album hit number 1 on the country charts that summer and gave Shania her first taste of crossover success. It wasn't just country fans who were clapping along to the song's unmistakable riff, which recalled the best of stadium rock, or line-dancing along to the more country-esque chorus. The song was an anthem for empowered women

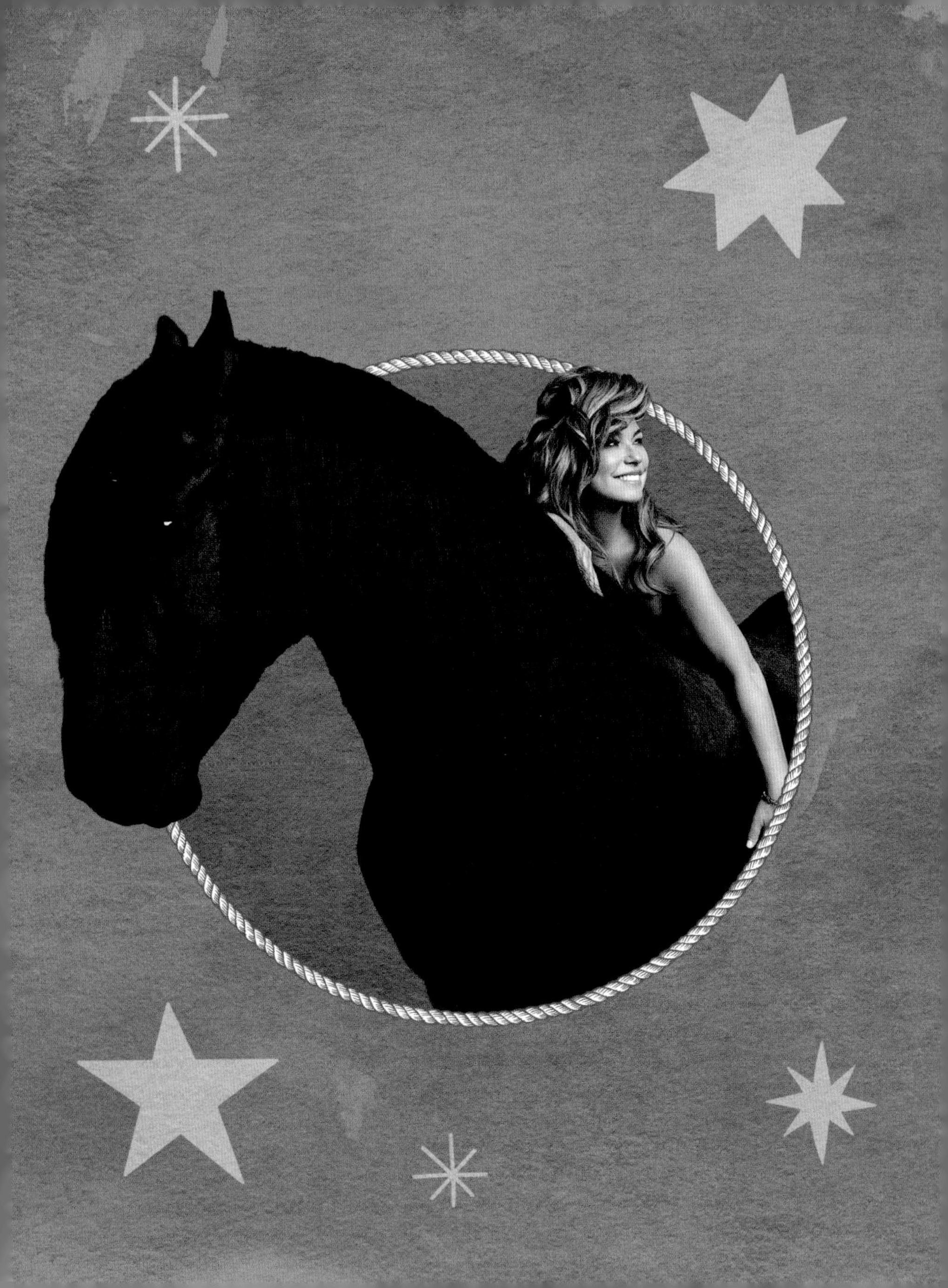

## BECAUSE, YUP, SHE IS REALLY HERDING CATTLE ON HORSEBACK IN THE "ANY MAN OF MINE" MUSIC VIDEO.

It would have been easy to fake it for the camera, but Shania took the opportunity to learn a new skill—one the enthusiastic ranch hand still uses to this day. Horses were her first big splurge after the massive success of *The Woman In Me*: five of them, named Shadow, Thunder, Tango, Dancer, and Alex.

who connected with the song's "Don't be afraid to lay down the law, ladies" message. In the video, Shania wears her take on the "Canadian tuxedo" (double denim): a cropped denim vest and jeans from her closet. But this time it wasn't a matter of budget, with the label more than happy to cough up for the newly crowned Queen of Country Pop.

To make the video for her third single "The Woman In Me (Needs the Man in You)," the whole team relocated to Cairo, Egypt, to shoot by the pyramids. Single number four, "(If You're Not in It for Love) I'm Outta Here!" was another unapologetic memo to badly behaved men—a warning to pickup artists to pack up and go home. It was also Shania's first international hit, charting at number 7 in Australia and providing an early taste of global dominance to come. The album won one award after another, and Shania performed at most of the big shows. She even opened the thirtieth annual Country Music Awards, performing an extra-spicy version of "Any Man of Mine," where she got her flirt on with the industry's finest: taking a quick pit stop on Travis Tritt's lap and tousling Johnny Cash's hair before taking the stage in pants and (what else?) a crop top.

## BECAUSE THE MAN KNEW A ONCE-IN-A-GENERATION TALENT WHEN HE SAW ONE.

**Spoiler alert** Mutt and Shania's love story did not last through the ages, but the legacy of their creative partnership remains. And there were a lot of good times. Lange was a famously press-shy and genre-agnostic producer whose fingerprints are all over the biggest 1980s and '90s jams from head-bangers ("Highway to Hell") to tearjerkers ("Everything I Do, I Do It for You"). At a time when Shania's talent needed a boost, Mutt came in like a turbocharger.

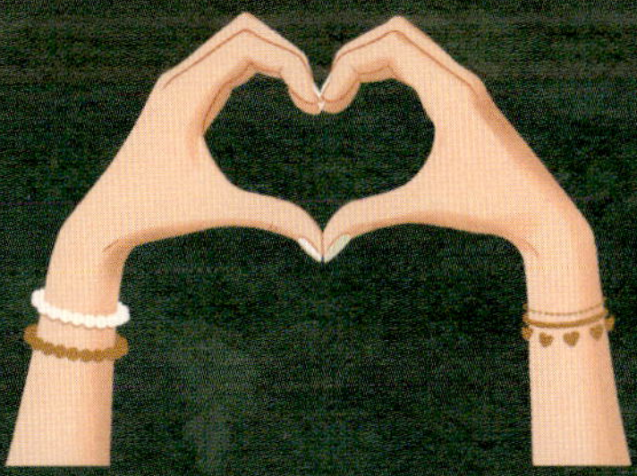

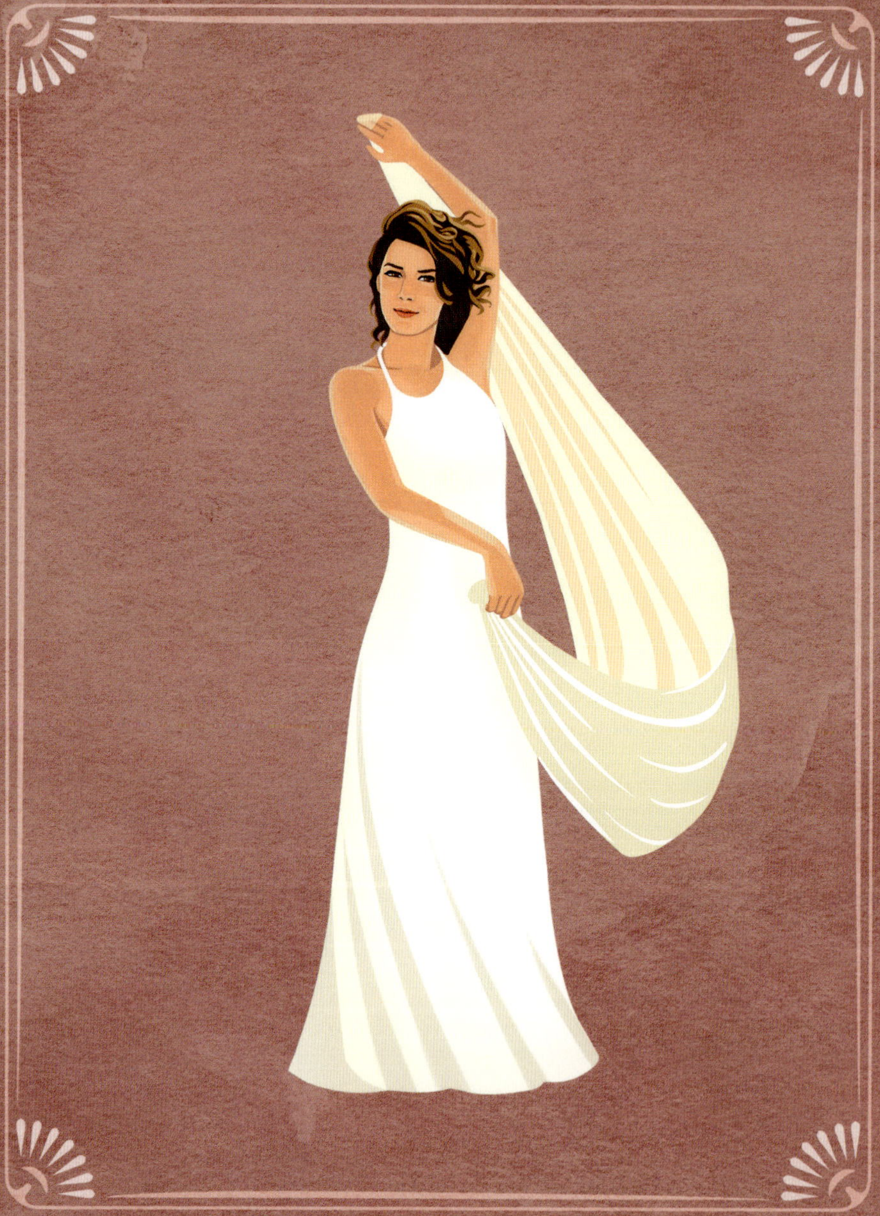

## BECAUSE WE'RE NOT IN TIMMINS ANYMORE.

Shania is one of very few artists to be granted permission to perform at the Egyptian pyramids (the only one of the original Seven Wonders of the World that still exists today). The Grateful Dead were the first Western act to perform there, in 1978. Since then the shortlist includes Sting, the Red Hot Chili Peppers, and Mariah Carey.

CHAPTER THREE

# Because She Became the Queen of (New) Country

“

Honey,
I’m home.

”

In some ways, success was a long time coming for Shania, who had been singing for more than twenty years before her first hit record. But in other ways it happened almost overnight: One day, she was a relative unknown who could go through day-to-day life with zero issues; the next, one of the world's most recognizable (and admired) faces. During a brief window of downtime after *The Woman In Me* exploded, she visited a mall in upstate New York with her sister Carrie Ann and her young nephew. The three of them were browsing from store to store when fans began to take notice. What started as an impromptu autograph session quickly devolved into a potentially dangerous mob, and mall security had to escort Shania and her family back to the car. (Pretty soon after that she hired a full-time security detail and adopted her beloved guard dog Tim, named for her hometown of Timmins.) There were aspects of success that Shania loved (seeing her songs embraced by millions, better wardrobe budgets), but the inability to blend into a crowd was not one of them. She once went incognito with her assistant on a shopping trip to Walmart just to get a taste of normalcy that was no longer part of her own existence.

But as much as her success in country music changed Shania's life, country music was also forever changed by Shania and her success at a time when Nashville was in transition. In 1985 the *New York Times* declared that country music was on its deathbed with Generation X turning to rock. By the next decade grunge was waiting at the gate: a new class of self-serious dudes in flannel (Nirvana, Pearl Jam, Stone Temple Pilots), whose angsty guitar anthems reflected the mood of the era. Hip-hop and R&B were also crossing over with huge mainstream hits by artists like Snoop Dogg, the Notorious B.I.G., and TLC. The country music of yore wasn't cutting it, so a group

### BECAUSE HER FACE IS NEARLY PERFECT—SCIENCE SAYS SO.

A 2009 study conducted by researchers at the University of Toronto endeavored to unpack the mathematics behind the "ideal" female face. Apparently, it all comes down to proportions (the distance between eyes and lips should be 36 percent of overall face length; the distance between pupils should be 46 percent of width), and turns out the closest IRL example of this so-called golden ratio is none other than a certain highly symmetrical singer from Canada. Shania scored higher than famously beautiful runners-up, including Angelina Jolie and Elizabeth Hurley.

of new artists—Garth Brooks, Alan Jackson, Travis Tritt—were taking a stab at reinvention, pumping out a sound that was country, yes, but also tipped its ten-gallon hat at the mass appeal of pop with catchy hooks and stadium-ready choruses. "New country" was the lifeline the genre needed but also a reason for traditionalists to clutch their bolo ties. And if the Grand Ole Opry types weren't sold

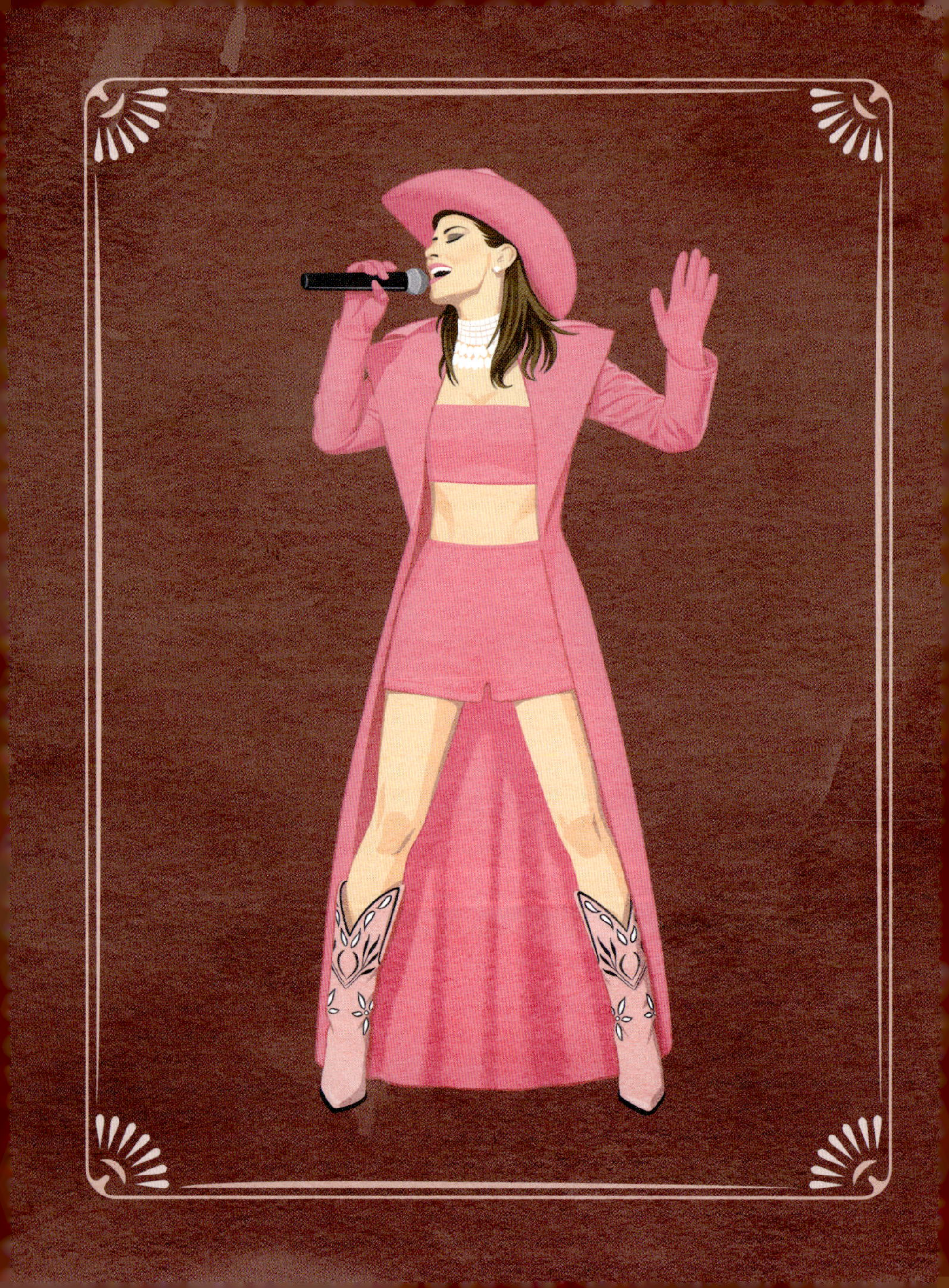

## BECAUSE BRING ON THE CANADIAN INVASION.

Shania wasn't the only northern light to hit it big during this musical era, which also included hit albums for Celine Dion, Sarah McLachlan, and Alanis Morissette.

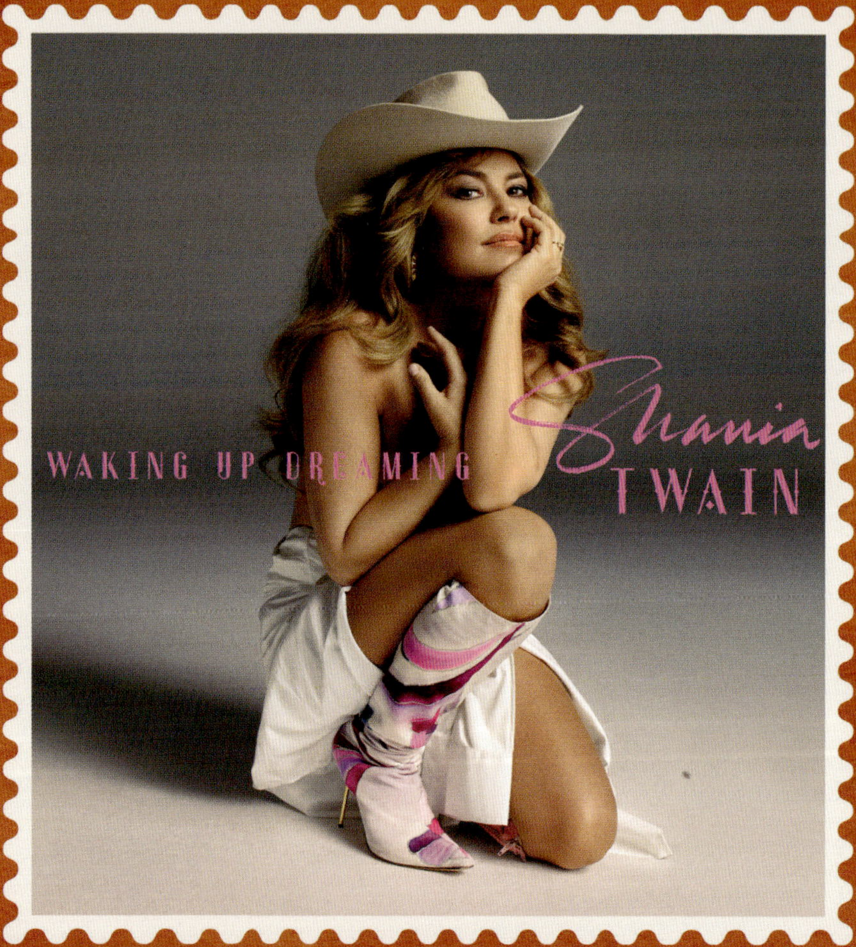
WAKING UP DREAMING
Shania
TWAIN

on a bunch of dudes working to widen the horizons of country music, they were downright scandalized by the female upstart from Canada who seemed to have tossed out the rule book (along with the bottom half of her top). How dare she write music that dismissed the idea of genre altogether? How dare she be so confident? How dare she dominate the country charts when she hadn't been born and bred by Nashville? And then, after it was clear audiences were embracing her, how dare she not follow the conventional wisdom where a hit album is followed up by a tour? Her fans were certainly eager to see her perform live, and her label wanted to send its rising star (and valuable asset) out on the road, pushing ticket sales. But Shania demonstrated her signature grit by going against expectation and returning to the studio, while Nashville went back to throwing shade: Perhaps her vocal chops just weren't up to snuff; maybe her sound was the product of a good editor. And then, when word got out that the follow-up album was costing more than half a million dollars (about double what was "standard" at the time), a whole new chorus of crap-talk arose, asking just who does this woman think she is?

The knives were out, but by that time Shania was hard at work, tucked away at her newly purchased hideaway in the Adirondacks: twenty square miles of land with a natural lake, snakes, and an electronic security gate. A lot of artists who experience celebrity for the first time are keen to check out all the Hollywood hot spots, but that was never Shania, who craved solitude and the great outdoors. Her first big splurge, other than the new real estate, was horses—five of them that she would ride in an effort to keep her head on straight amid the mounting pressure of celebrity. The success of *The Woman In Me* had exceeded every imaginable metric, and even fans were wondering if it was possible to live up to such a massive smash. Turns out it was more of a warm-up act. Next stop: world domination.

## BECAUSE, MAN, DID SHE SHOW THEM.

The album that cost $500,000 to make went on to make millions and millions more with the Come On Over tour alone grossing over $70 million.

Between records, Shania signed a new manager (the guy behind Bruce Springsteen's explosion) and set out a three-point game plan: (1) crossover success, (2) penetration of the global market, (3) touring. That first objective was already well in the works. "Any Man of Mine" had hit number 31 on the *Billboard* Hot 100. The first single off *Come On Over*, an up-tempo fiddle-heavy favorite called "Love Gets Me Every Time," did even better, reaching number 25. But it was the album's third single, "You're Still the One" that changed everything—an autobiographical ode to Shania and Mutt that was a response to the critics who said he married her face and she married his industry status. And yet, all these years (okay, fine, *four* years) later, here they were "still together, still going strong."

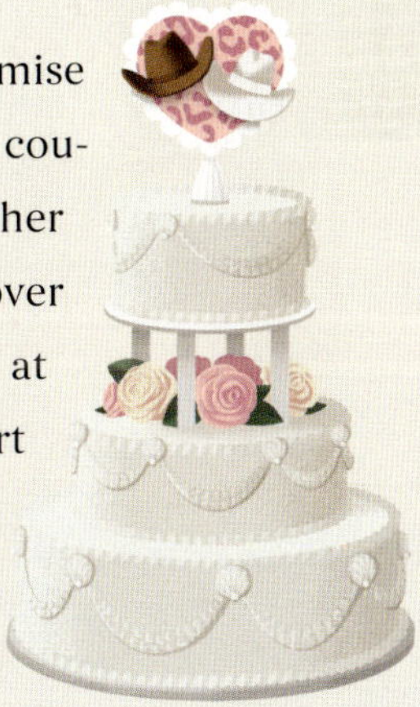

**Spoiler alert** The song's premise may not have held up for this particular couple in the long run, but millions of other couples have embraced the sentiment over the years, and the song's eight weeks at the top of the Adult Contemporary Chart established Shania among the era's biggest names. And the hits just kept on coming. "From This Moment On"

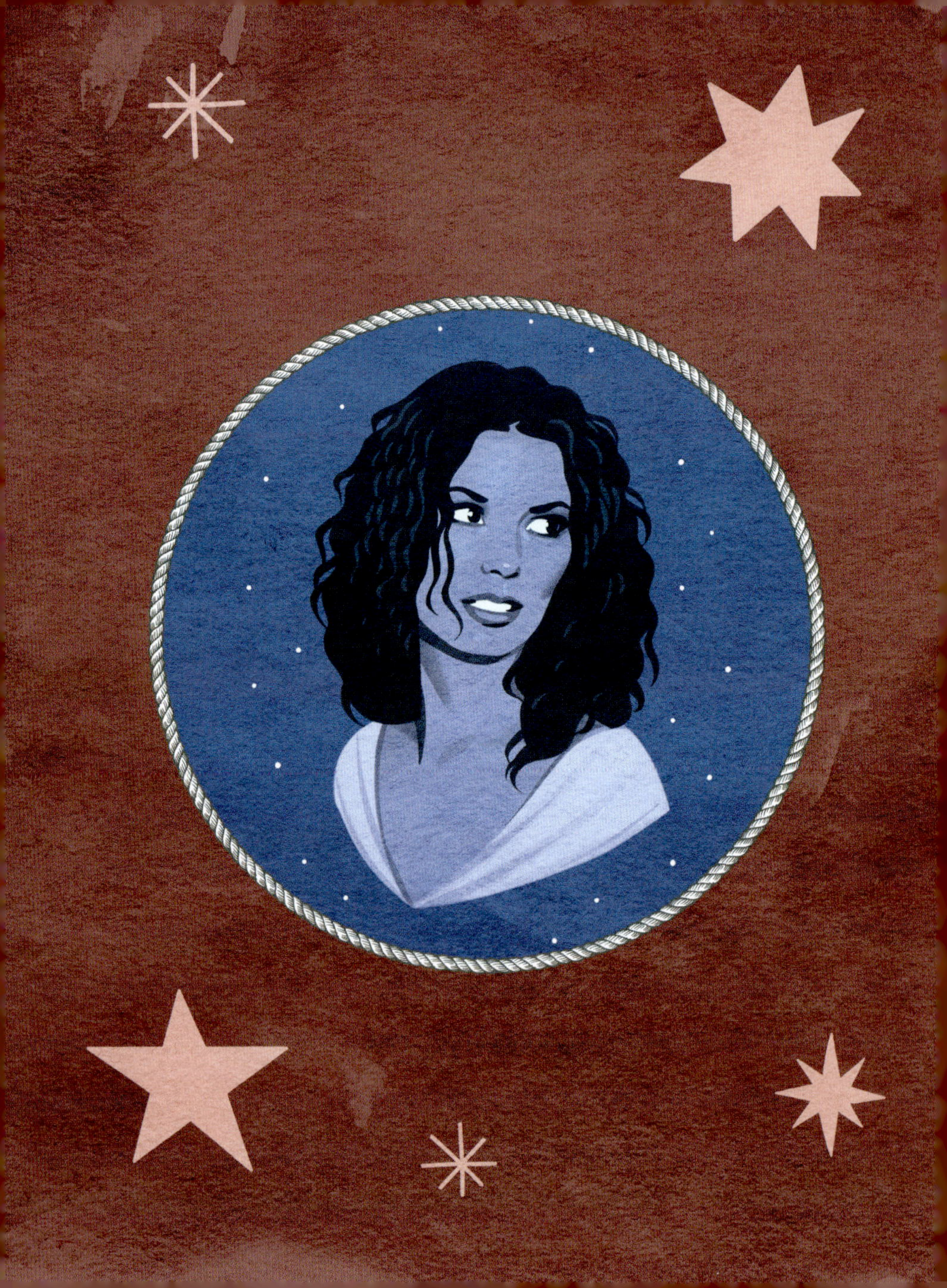

## BECAUSE GOL DARN IT: SHE KNOWS HOW TO WRITE A HIT.

Shania had a different title in mind for her 1997 track "Love Gets Me Every Time." She wanted to call it "Gol Darn Gone and Done It," after the country world expression that is a more SFW way to say goddamn. That didn't happen but the phrase features prominently in the lyrics.

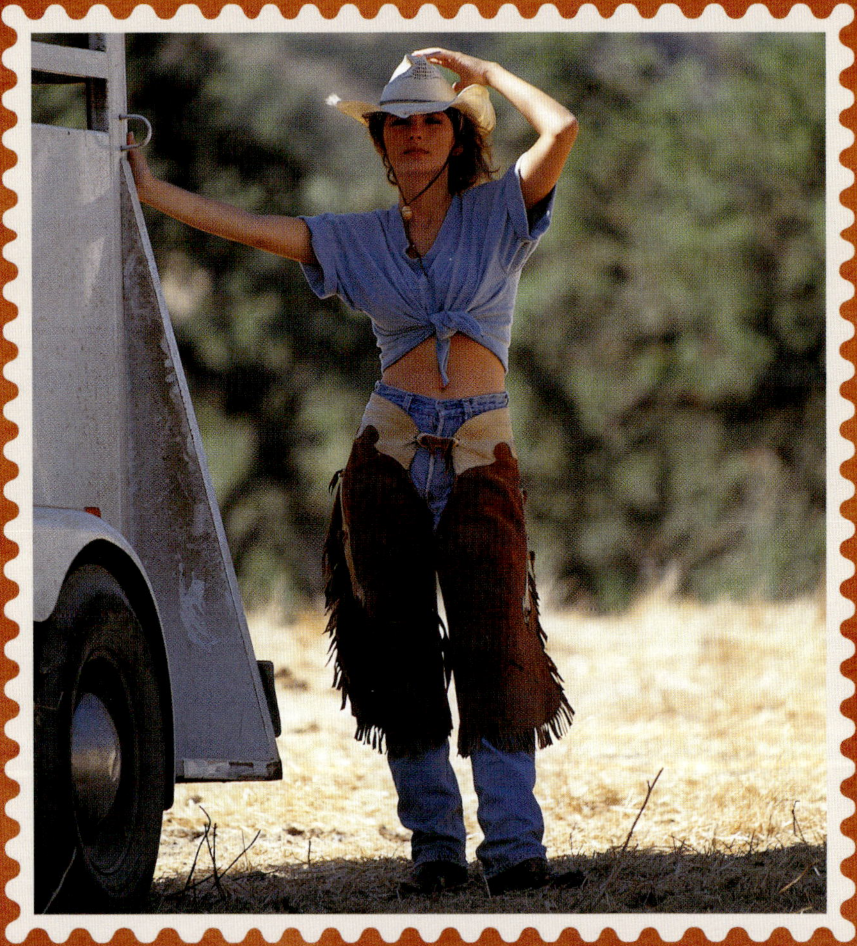

**BECAUSE SHE OUT-BOSSED THE BOSS.**

*Born in the U.S.A.* was a massive success, selling more than 30 million copies and ranking number 23 among the top-selling albums of all time. *Come On Over* sold 40 million copies and comes in at number 8.

was another slow song, and not one Shania initially envisioned singing herself. She had imagined the power ballad as a possibility for her fellow diva and CanCon Queen Celine Dion, who was achieving an almost parallel success to Shania with her 1996 blockbuster *Falling into You*. But Mutt convinced Shania to give it a go, and the result became the ultimate wedding "first dance" staple.

With "From This Moment On" burning up the charts and a slew of equally iconic hit singles set to follow it, Shania was finally ready to take her show on the road, and even the highest expectations for her live show were blown up by the Come On Over tour's ample supply of pyrotechnics. Then, in Detroit, Shania sold out the Pine Knob Music Theatre in just twenty-nine minutes—a pace

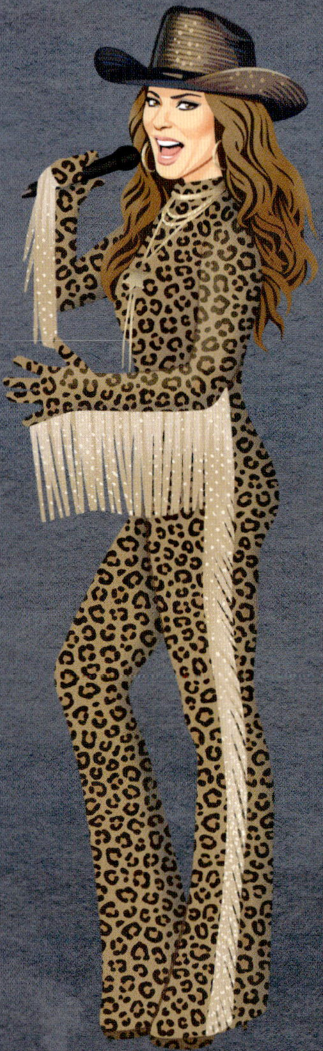

## BECAUSE SHE'S NOT A DIVA, BUT SHE WAS A DIVA.

As in the 1998 VH1 concert special *Divas*, which featured Shania as a member of Musical Mount Rushmore, alongside Aretha Franklin, Mariah Carey, Gloria Estefan, and Celine Dion. Shania has said that her best memory of the epic evening took place before the show when she invited her fellow divas onto her bus to rehearse. That and the big hair.

matched only by the Who, Metallica, Bob Seger, and Jimmy Buffett—and continued with stops all over Canada, the rest of North America, and four dates in Europe.

Shania took a night off for the 1999 Grammys, where *Come On Over* was nominated for six awards. The night included wins for Best Female Country Performance and Best Country Song. She also delivered the night's most memorable live performance with her signature hit, "Man! I Feel Like a Woman!" And, man, did the rest of the world feel like Shania. The Come On Over tour was the most successful tour ever by a female artist up to that time and the album would eventually become the most successful album by a solo female artist in any genre at any time ever.

CHAPTER FOUR

# Because, Man, What a Woman

"Let's go, girls."

When Shania first came up with the spoken intro line to her chart-climbing, career-defining mega-hit "Man! I Feel Like a Woman!", she had no idea that the phrase, and the entire song, would become a rallying cry—an anthem for female empowerment and an acknowledgment of the multitudes contained in every modern woman and in Shania herself. As a kid, she was uncomfortable with her nascent femininity (she would tape down her chest to avoid attention), and even as an adult she remains at least semi-prudish ("at a nude beach, I'm wearing a cover-up," she once told

**BECAUSE ONLY ICONS QUOTE THEMSELVES.**

"Let me start by saying, 'Let's go, girls!'" Shania said in her speech accepting the Equal Play Award at the 2023 CMT Awards, in recognition of her contributions to diversity in country music.

a reporter). But onstage she was a boss, a babe, a vamp, a vixen, 360 degrees of a woman in control of her sexuality and unwilling to make any apologies for that. She was enjoying every minute, radical in her commitment to keeping things positive. At the time, women in pop were a chaotic mix of sexy schoolgirls (see Britney Spears) and angry alt rockers (see Alanis Morissette). The former, we can now see as deeply problematic; the latter, deeply necessary, but so was Shania, offering a take on feminism that was appealing in its optimism: "The best thing about being a woman," goes the chorus of "Man! I Feel Like a Woman!" is the prerogative to "have a little fun."

No big surprise that this was not an attitude embraced by establishment purists of the time. Pre-Shania, country music was as restrictive when it came to gender as it was when it came to genre. Outlaw types like Johnny Cash and Waylon Jennings were beloved for their songs about sex and drugs and gunfire, but, for women, the range of acceptable subject matter and behavior was a lot more narrow. The women in country lyrics were either homemakers or homewreckers, and women singing country were expected to preach and practice traditional values. And, of course, to look exactly the right amount of pretty.

Going back to the early days of her first album release, Shania got used to fielding questions that focused on her looks rather than her records or her songwriting chops. Her sex appeal was forever at the center of the conversation, and after she and Mutt started writing hits together there arose speculation that *he* was the talented songwriter, the Svengali figure behind a pretty face and perfectly toned set of abs. Never mind that many of their hits were songs Shania had started writing way back at her cottage in Ontario, or that the husband-and-wife duo share writing credits on all their collaborations. The idea that she could be both gorgeous *and* extremely talented simply did not align with the one-dimensional depictions of womanhood that were prevalent at the time. The country singer Steve Earle famously called Shania "America's highest paid lap

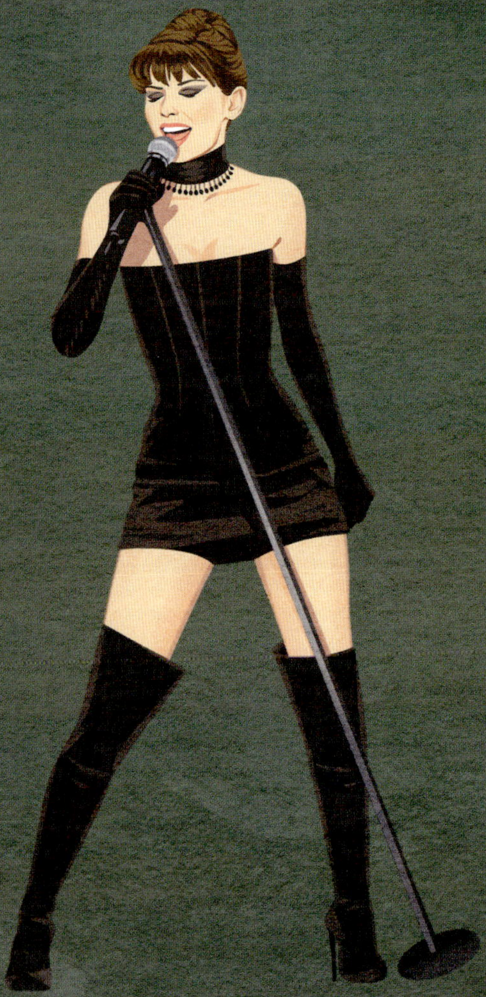

## BECAUSE OF COURSE WE GOT IT.

When the execs at her label first heard the lyrics to "Man! I Feel Like a Woman!" they worried that everyday women wouldn't "get" it. This was not terribly surprising since underestimating women was integral to the music industry DNA at that point. But the best part about being Shania after the Grammy-winning, chart-topping success of *The Woman In Me* was the prerogative to go ahead with the track anyway. And, needless to say, the women in the world more than understood what she was saying.

**BECAUSE BLESS HIS HEART.**

That's country for *kiss my ascent up the charts*. Shania never responded to Earle's diss directly, instead pointing out the obvious following the smash success of *The Woman In Me*: "It takes more than a belly button to sell eight million records."

dancer." The so-called defender of "classic country" had a poster of her on the door of his dressing room with the word *talent* beside an arrow pointing to her belly button. The haters only got louder as our girl got more successful, her shows got bigger, and her costumes embraced high fashion and various other influences that were more MTV than Grand Ole Opry, but Shania wasn't about to give in. Her approach to gender stereotypes was not so different from her dismissal of traditional music categories: You can take your labels and stuff 'em.

By the 1999 Grammy Awards, it had started to feel like the music world may have finally gotten the message. The show that year was dubbed the "Year of the Woman" because all the biggest categories were dominated by

**BECAUSE IT WAS NEVER ABOUT BRAD PITT.**

Shania was working on the lyrics for "That Don't Impress Me Much" in 1995 at the same time as the paparazzi leaked nude photos of Pitt on a vacation with his then-girlfriend Gwyneth Paltrow. The world went crazy, but Shania was all—what's the big deal? Hasn't everyone seen a naked body before?

female nominees. Shania lost out on the night's biggest prize, Album of the Year, to Lauryn Hill, although Hill's historic win (the first hip-hop album to win in the pop category) pointed to the post-genre universe that Shania had helped to create. And she brought the house down with a mid-show performance of "Man! I Feel Like a Woman!" capturing the energy and power of the sisterhood. Not that you'd know it from the way the media pitted these industry powerhouses against each other.

Move over, Shania, declared the headline on a 1999 profile of Faith Hill, as if the charts could only accommodate

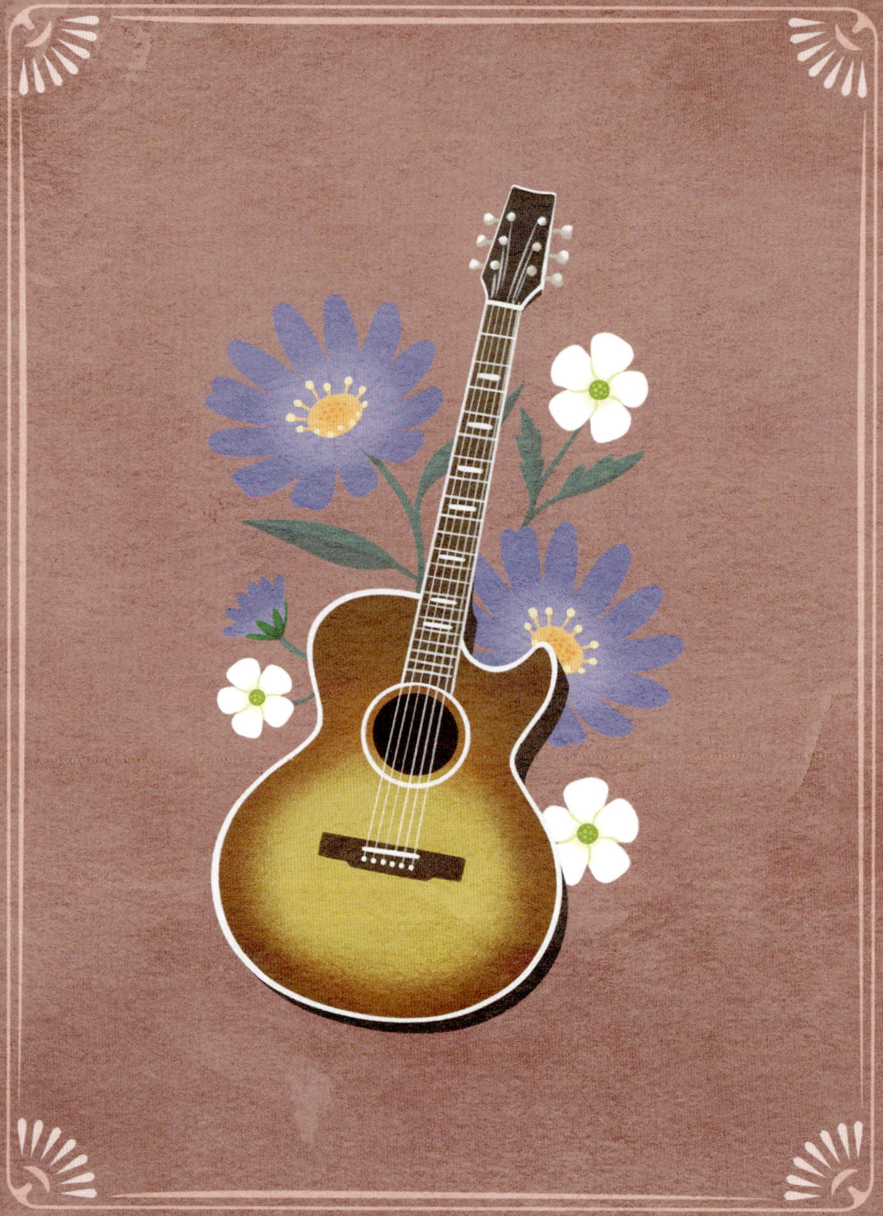

## BECAUSE WHO ELSE COULD RHYME "DISTRESSED" WITH "PMS"?

If you thought crop tops were scandalous . . . "Honey, I'm Home" (1997) was the first song to explicitly discuss female menstruation on the country airwaves.

one hit-making woman at a time. As inaccurate as these tropes were (see also: Women don't want to listen to other women on the radio; listeners will change the channel if you play two female artists back-to-back), they made it hard for female artists to get the radio play they deserved. Enter Shania to change everything with one infinitely catchy, slyly subversive hit at a time. The music got everyone out on the dance floor while the lyrics served up a fresh and assertive counterpoint to country's long-held "Stand By Your Man" mantra.

"Any Man of Mine" was cheeky and flirty, but also a full-on feminist manifesto from a woman who knew how she deserved to be treated and wasn't afraid to spell it out. On "Honey, I'm Home," the housewife stereotype is upended by a woman who arrives home after a hard day at work and wants her guy to get her a cold one and rub her feet. "If You Wanna Touch Her, Ask!" advocated for consent decades before the #MeToo movement. And of course "That Don't Impress Me Much" is the ultimate send-up of mediocre dude-dom that included a playful swipe at the biggest hunk on

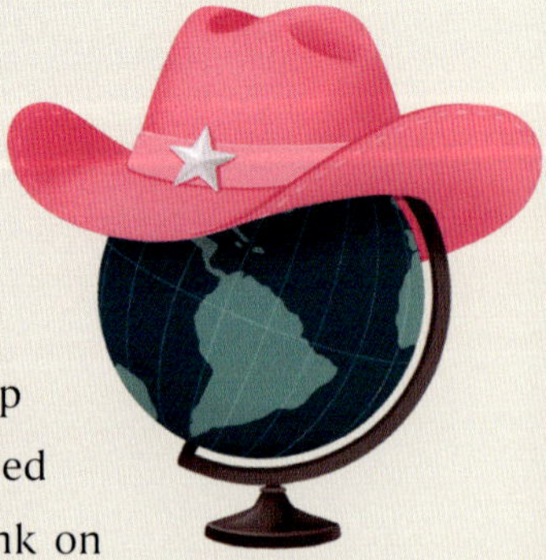

**BECAUSE THE REST OF THE WORLD WAS PLENTY IMPRESSED.**

"That Don't Impress Me Much" was Shania's first truly global hit, charting in Australia, Austria, Belgium, Canada, Finland, Germany, Hungary, Ireland, Latvia, Netherlands, New Zealand, Norway, Scotland, Sweden, Switzerland, and the United Kingdom.

the planet. And possibly the greatest music video ever made.

For Shania, the visual aspects of performance were a chance to look awesome, yes, but also to express her artistry and further amplify her message. Consider the music video for "That Don't Impress Me Much," which underscores the lyrics of the song by setting the story in the Mojave Desert. So not only is Shania unimpressed with these suitors (the brainiac, the babe, the guy with the car), but she's hitchhiking in the middle of the desert and she *still* isn't willing to let them pick her up. The same video marked the zenith of two very important collaborations in Shania's life: one with the fashion designer Marc Bouwer and another with leopard print. This particular hooded velvet bodysuit is the look that launched ten thousand Halloween costumes and was later on display at the Country Music Hall of Fame and Museum in Nashville, along with the top hat and tails look from "Man! I Feel Like a Woman!" which was also Marc Bouwer's creation.

So many of Shania's hits were about upending and redefining gender roles. With "Man! I Feel Like a Woman!" she pushes the boundaries even further. The song was inspired by the time she spent in drag bars in Toronto in her early twenties, where the fashion and the makeup were always on point. And also by the iconic video for

### BECAUSE YOU CAN'T ACHIEVE ARTISTIC EXCELLENCE IF YOU'RE EXHAUSTED.

The drive into the desert to shoot the video for "That Don't Impress Me Much" was ninety minutes each way, so when the crew headed back to civilization, Shania opted to camp out and save the hours for sleeping.

**BECAUSE THE MUSE/MAESTRO RELATIONSHIP IS BASED ON TRUST.**

Shania came to trust her fashion fairy godfather implicitly following their first video collab for "From This Moment On." She wanted her hair to be big, but he insisted on a sleek, tied-back look to complement the simplicity of her silver turtleneck dress. He won, and the iconic image speaks for itself.

Robert Palmer's mid-eighties hit "Addicted to Love," where the backup band is a group of nameless female supermodels. Shania did the whole thing in reverse, fronting a band of boy-bots and starting off in a top hat and tails and then slowly removing layers. The visual impact was instant iconography but, under all that pomp, Shania is exploring the idea that expressions of gender and sexuality can be whatever you want them to be: "Men's shirts, short skirts" (*oh-oh-oh*). Between the inclusive politics and the A-plus lewks, it's no surprise that Shania found a huge fan base in the LGBTQ+ community, just as country music was about to turn back the clock on progress.

### BECAUSE SHANIA HEARTS DRAG QUEENS.

As well as finding big inspo in drag fashion, Shania has voiced her support for the drag community, often featuring drag performers in her live shows, appearing on *RuPaul's Drag Race*, and speaking out against anti-drag legislation.

Shania's success was key in forging a path for so many women in country who came after her: Faith Hill, LeAnn Rimes, Martina McBride, and the Dixie Chicks (later known as the Chicks), but then 9/11 happened and country music saw a dramatic return to its more old-school, bro-centric roots (the land of the free, the home of the brave, and all the strong, straight, sometimes gun-toting white men to uphold those values). Once again, women were being edged out, and when the Chicks famously spoke out against George W. Bush's invasion of Iraq in 2003, the backlash was explosive. And that same scenario is still playing out more than twenty years later with a resurgence of country songs catering to an outdated (and offensive) "good old boy" mentality. It's all about themes and lyrics, but also airtime. Even with so much exceptional talent, women in country still struggle for radio play and Shania is still advocating whenever she can.

In 2023 she was the Equal Play Award honoree at the CMT awards, which pays tribute to champions of gender equality. "When I wrote the phrase 'Man! I Feel Like a Woman!' I had no idea it would become the undercurrent of a decades-long career," she said, while accepting her award. "It's amazing how just one statement can empower so many. [The song] has been adopted by an array of fantastic communities all around the world and become a genuine path of power and progress."

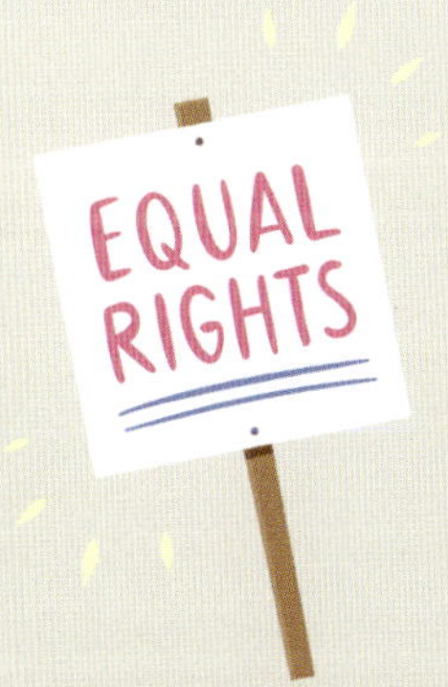

CHAPTER FIVE

# Because What Didn't Kill Her Made Her Kick Butt

“

I'm gonna get you while I've got you in sight. I'm gonna get you if it takes all night.

”

Bro country was making a comeback in the early aughts, but the Queen of Country Pop had transcended genre and her dominance was unlike anything the music world had witnessed before. When her fourth album, *Up!*, was released at the end of 2002, it debuted at number 1 on both the country charts and the *Billboard* 200—a first for Shania who had, by now, easily crossed "top touring artist" and "international superstar" off her to-do list and cemented her crossover artist status. So much so that *Up!* was recorded and released in three different musical styles with color-coded cover art: Green for country, red for pop, and blue for international dance.

In 2003, Shania was the first country artist ever to headline the Super Bowl halftime show. Not that there was anything explicitly country about her high-octane set, which also included performances by No Doubt and Sting. Shania opened the show with "Man! I Feel Like a Woman!" dressed in a rhinestone bra and leather cutout dress because she "didn't want to look too mumsy."

She was, by this time, a mom. Shania and Mutt welcomed their son, Eja D'Angelo Lange, in August of 2001. The Come On Over tour had wrapped up a ridiculously successful run at the end of 1999 and for the first time in almost a decade, Shania had time to devote herself

**BECAUSE WHEN YOUR MOM IS SHANIA TWAIN, YOUR LULLABIES ARE ORIGINALS.**

Shania once performed the sweet song that she wrote to sing her baby to sleep on a British talk show: "Eja D / Can you count to one, two, three . . ."

**BECAUSE SHE GOT THE WHOLE WORLD ON THE DANCE FLOOR.**

The music on the *Up!* international version was partly recorded in Mumbai and heavily influenced by the sounds and style of Bollywood, featuring instruments like the sitar and the dholak. Shania has said that her favorite song from that album is the international remix of "When You Kiss Me."

to a different dream: being a parent. She and Mutt had moved from upstate New York to Switzerland. The goal was to escape the kind of paparazzi-hunted, fishbowl existence that had grown ever more intense with Shania's increasing success. After considering several locations in Europe, they chose the shores of Lake Geneva because nobody there seemed to care much about an IRL icon in their midst. (Also, the spectacular views of the Swiss Alps didn't hurt.) Becoming a mom was reorienting for Shania, who worked on *Up!* during her baby's downtime, often while he napped in the studio. Shania was 100 percent devoted to her little boy,

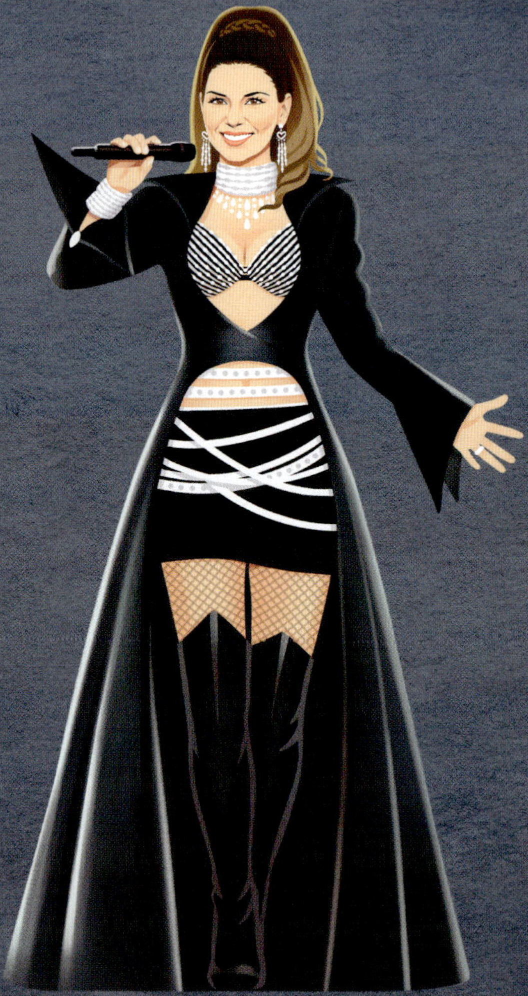

### BECAUSE LET'S GO, FOOTBALL FANS!

Twain got the crowd at Qualcomm Stadium in San Diego on their feet with a two-song set, starting with "Man! I Feel Like a Woman!" and ending with "Up!"—a song title she took quite literally, rising above the stage on an elevated platform that lifted her up (up, up—and away) at the end of her performance.

and when it was time to go out on tour, mother and son hit the road together. Shania had signed with new management now—Q Prime, a company most famous for its work with Metallica and other heavy-metal acts, and the resulting tour was (to use her words) a "big-ass rock show," including a pyrotechnic budget that was up there with the GDP of a small country. But with ticket sales nearing $100 million, she could afford to spare no expense. The album itself achieved diamond status (that is, going platinum ten times over), making Shania the only artist in history to do this three times back-to-back-to-back. (She still holds that distinction as of

**BECAUSE THE VIDEO FOR "I'M GONNA GET YOU GOOD" WAS AMONG THE MOST EXPENSIVE EVER MADE.**

At the time, it was rumored to have cost $6 million. In it Shania plays a bodysuited space alien on a motorbike who fights a flying robot.

2025.) "Up, up up—there's nowhere but up from here," went the title track's chorus and for a second there, things actually felt that way.

It was during the Up! tour that Shania first started to experience a troubling health issue: millisecond blackouts that left her dizzy and discombobulated onstage. She would later find out that this was a symptom of Lyme disease she had contracted from a tick bite that she got while out horseback riding in 2003. But in the moment, she had no idea what was wrong with her—only that this mysterious affliction was also having an impact on

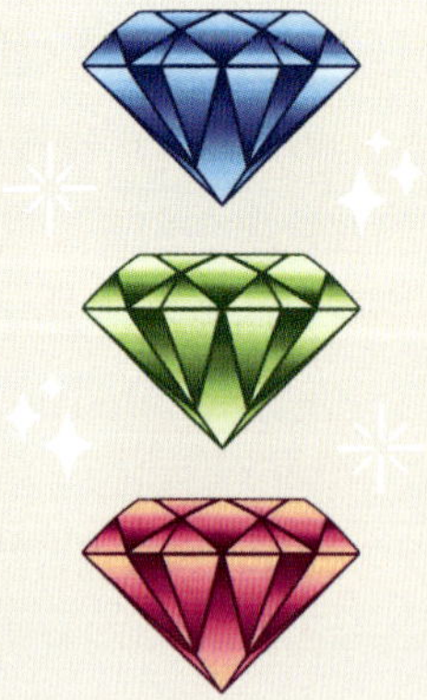

her voice. Plans to record a new album were shelved as Shania worried that her essential instrument might never come back to her.

Of course she was terrified and in need of support. It was the sort of crisis where having a spouse/creative partner should have been a comfort. But by the time the Up! tour was over, her relationship with Mutt was as strained as her vocal cords. She worried that all the time apart (with her on the road and him in the studio) had caused them to grow apart, and she confided this concern to the woman who had become her closest friend in Switzerland. Marie-Anne was Mutt's assistant, and she

### BECAUSE THE SONGS STOOD THE TEST OF TIME (EVEN IF THE ROMANCE DIDN'T).

For Shania, the decade between 1994 and 2005 encompassed three chart-topping records, two blockbuster tours, and too many love songs to list. Shania's first marriage didn't end up being her happily ever after, but the music isn't going anywhere.

## BECAUSE SHE WROTE HER WAY OUT OF DESPAIR.

The first song that Shania wrote after her split from Mutt Lange and several years away from music actually began as a mantra: "Today is your day" is something Shania would repeat to herself every morning as she struggled to put herself back together and rediscover her voice. Her songwriting process is documented in her 2011 reality series *Why Not? with Shania Twain* and the uplifting track ended up serving as the show's theme song.

and Shania had bonded when they were both pregnant and had babies on the same timeline. Only Marie-Anne was also the third party in a love triangle that would bring about the implosion of two separate marriages and one of the most successful professional collaborations in music history.

This double betrayal was devastating. Shania only got out of bed in the morning to take care of her son.

Her heart was in pieces and her voice wasn't doing much better. She spent years visiting doctors all over the world, none of whom could explain what was happening. It wasn't until 2011 that she first heard the term *dysphonia*, a condition that causes the nerves to tighten around the vocal cords. Lyme disease had made her vulnerable, but the dysphonia was neurological, related to the stress of her recent hardship but also stemming from a life's worth of unaddressed trauma.

When Shania first became famous, there were journalists who suggested that the rags part of her rags-to-riches narrative was something she had exaggerated for the purposes of marketing, but, if anything, the opposite was true. Country music is a magnet for sob stories, but there are few artists who can top Shania in terms of overcoming difficult circumstances. Her survival story begins with a childhood that was plagued not only by poverty but also by mental illness and abuse. She was a witness to domestic violence when her father would beat

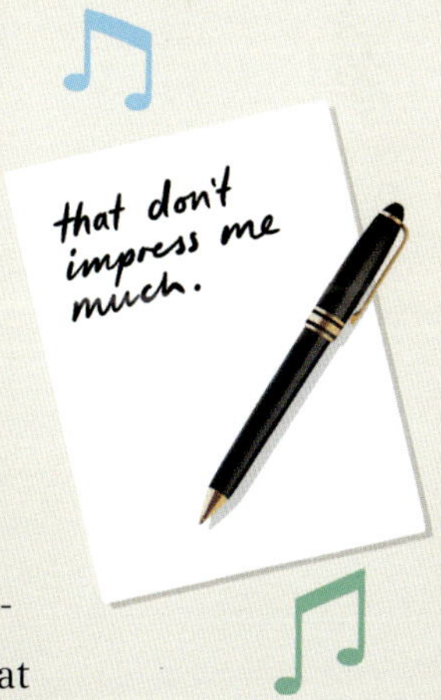

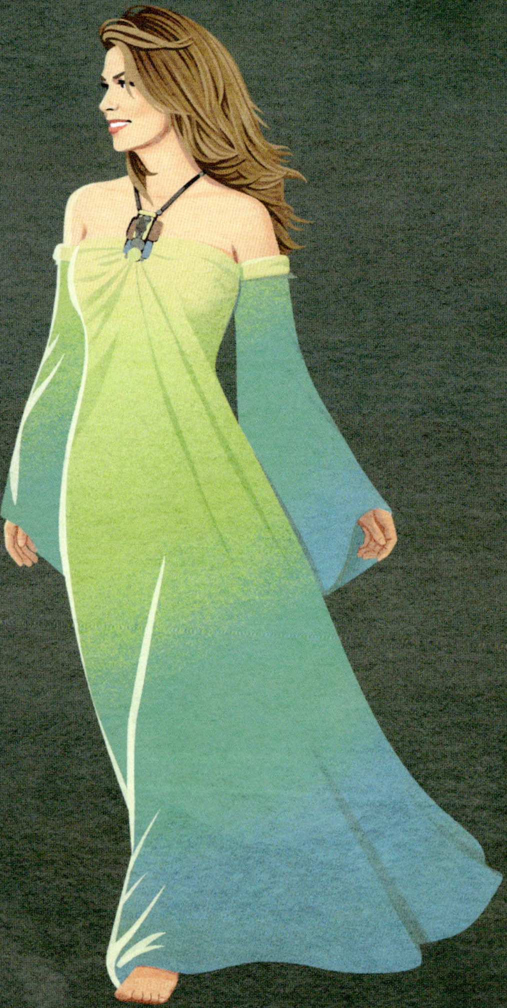

**BECAUSE REVENGE IS A DISH BEST SERVED IN A LIME-GREEN SARONG.**

In the gloriously unsubtle video for "Life's About to Get Good," Shania goes from bummed out in her pj's to blissed-out on a beach. "Time to forget you forever," she sings, while looking at a picture of herself and her ex (before the guy falls out of the picture).

her mother on a regular basis, and endured sexual abuse perpetrated by the same man—something she revealed for the first time in her 2011 memoir, *From This Moment On*. For so long, the singular focus placed on succeeding in and then sustaining her career had meant turning away from any emotional difficulty, but Mutt's betrayal broke that dam and there was no turning back.

There was also no quick fix. The world's most successful recording artist had taken a break in 2004, but she had never intended to stay away so long. Her fans wondered what had happened, and when news of her divorce hit the tabloids, speculation went into overdrive. The desire to reclaim her own narrative inspired

Shania to write her memoir. Her dream of inspiring others along their own healing journeys resulted in her own Oprah-produced reality docuseries. *Why Not? with Shania Twain* followed Shania as she worked to regain her confidence and her voice, which had slowly started to come back with therapy and rest. She had even managed to write and record a new song—a gentle guitar track called "Today Is Your Day."

### BECAUSE THIS GUY IS AN IRL DISNEY PRINCE.

After almost a year of being together, Fred organized a surprise trip up into the glaciers in Verbier, Switzerland. When they arrived, Shania saw a red heart spray-painted into the snow, surrounded by red roses, with a bottle of pink champagne chilling nearby. Fred got down on one knee and presented her with an engraved watch. Not a marriage proposal, but a proposal to let him love her. Sorry, Mutt *who*?

**BECAUSE TALK ABOUT EPIC.**

The Vegas stage show included fake snow, two horses, and a motorcycle.

It was a little easier to have a sunny outlook now that her personal life was in a better place. Frédéric Thiébaud was a Swiss businessman who had been the one to first inform Shania about the affair going on between his wife and her husband. The first time they hung out afterwards, she sat in his kitchen for five hours without saying a single word and certainly love was the last thing on her mind. At first Shania saw Fred as

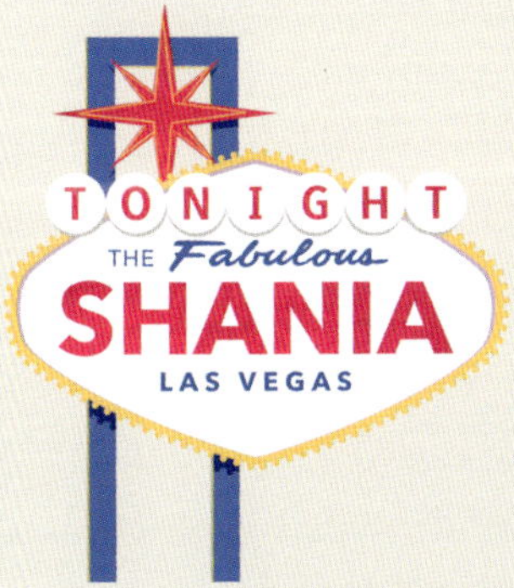

### BECAUSE YOU'RE NOT A MUSIC ICON UNTIL YOU HAVE STAGED A FAUX FAREWELL TOUR.

Like Cher and Elton John and so many other enduring artists before her, Shania launched a "farewell tour" that ended up being more of a comeback vehicle. The Rock This Country tour marked her first time hitting the road in more than a decade, and by the time she was finished, goodbye was officially off the table.

the only person who could really understand what she was going through, and their early conversations were around their common heartbreak. But, eventually, what started as a trauma bond became a real friendship and, soon after, a lot more. After dating for a year, the couple got married in Puerto Rico on New Year's Day, with their wedding date (1-1-11) perfectly articulating a fresh start.

A resuscitation of her singing career was also in the works. Shania recorded a Christmas duet with Michael Bublé in 2011. That same year Lionel Richie convinced her to rerecord a duet of his classic romantic anthem "Endless Love." Her voice was not the same as it had been, but with plenty of care and preparation, she was starting to sound pretty amazing. And, of course, this is Shania we're talking about, so the comeback was never going to be low-key.

It was a Las Vegas first in November 2012, when the main drag was closed to traffic so that more than forty horses could parade up to the iconic fountain outside of Caesars Palace. At the end of the procession—also on horseback—was Shania, quite literally back in the saddle and ready to take Sin City by storm. If Vegas residencies had become a bit of a career graveyard in the 1980s and '90s, the grand tradition had gotten a modern revamp, courtesy of Shania's fellow Canadian Celine Dion, who started performing *A New Day. . .* at Caesars Palace in 2003. Performing in a fixed location was a chance to make the spectacle that much bigger. *Shania Twain: Still the One* was another big-ass rock show, a 100-minute dance party, a no-apologies nostalgia-fest and proof that Shania was ready to reclaim her place in the spotlight (and in a manufactured snowfall).

The Vegas residency ran for three years, followed by a North American tour that was originally billed as

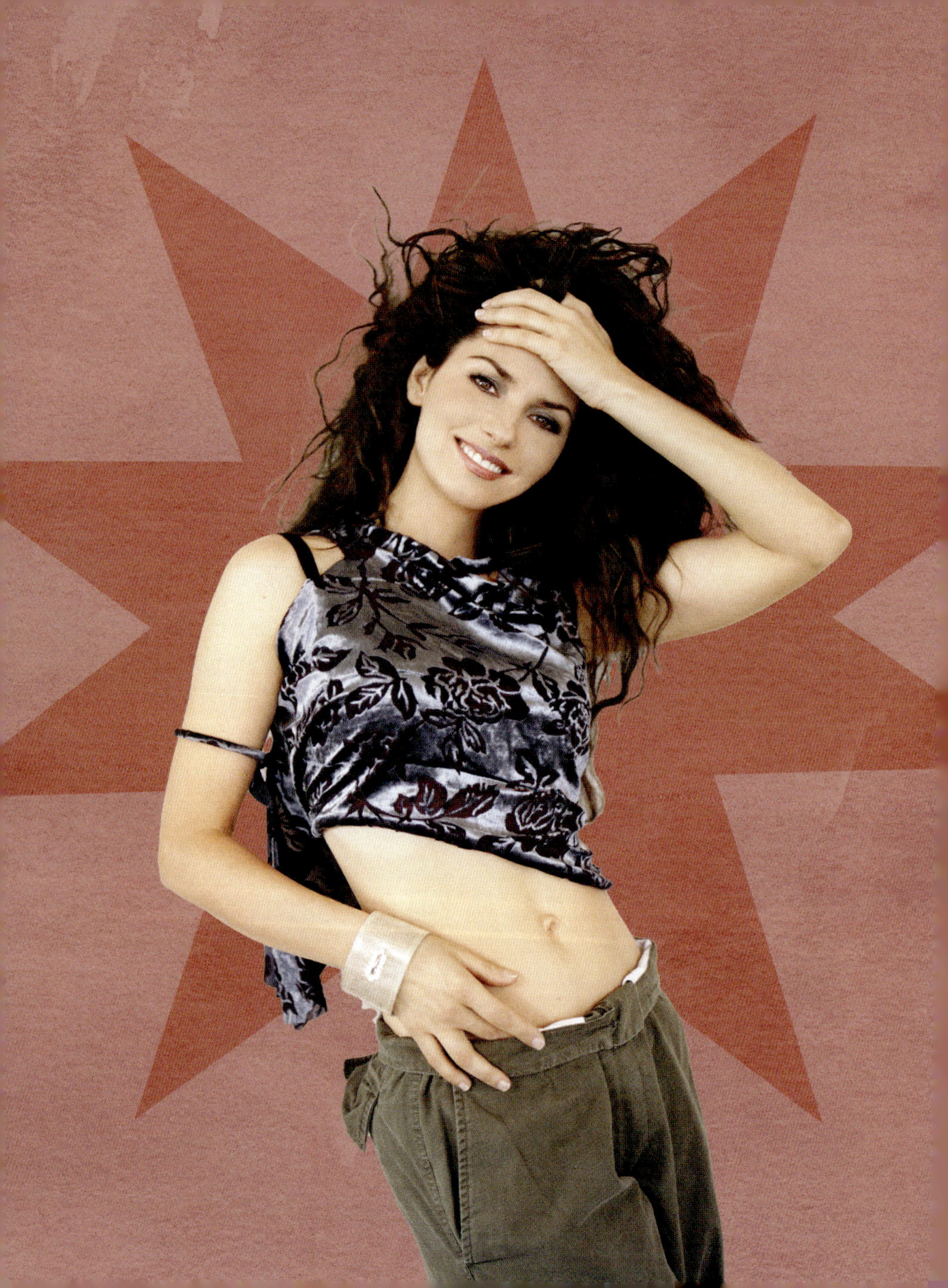

**BECAUSE SHE'S NOT MAKING ANY APOLOGIES.**

Accepting her CMT Lifetime Achievement Award, Shania thanked her "first booking agent," her mom, who got her gigs in bars and sometimes strip clubs, explaining, "We didn't have the Mickey Mouse Club then."

a farewell. In 2016 she picked up the Lifetime Achievement Award from Country Music Television, and in 2017 she was finally ready to release new music. Her first album since the split with Mutt was called *Now*, based on the idea of living in the moment, rather than dwelling on the past. "Life's about to get good," she sang on the album's infectious, fabulously feel-good and just-the-right-amount-of-sass opening single, and—finally!—she was right.

CHAPTER SIX

# Because She Is the Ultimate Music World Auntie

"I'm havin' a party. A party for two."

The "Mama Said" TikTok challenge in 2021 was set to the lyrics of Lukas Grange's 2015 hit: "Mama said it was okay/Mama said it was quite alright." The idea was that artists could give props to their creative "parents"—the rule breakers and ceiling smashers whose work had paved the way for their own. And when Taylor Swift decided to get in on the fun, she didn't leave any question as to who "Mama" is. "They said country girls can't do pop" wrote the post-genre icon before cutting to an image of Shania in full "Man! I Feel Like a Woman!" regalia. The post (which inspired

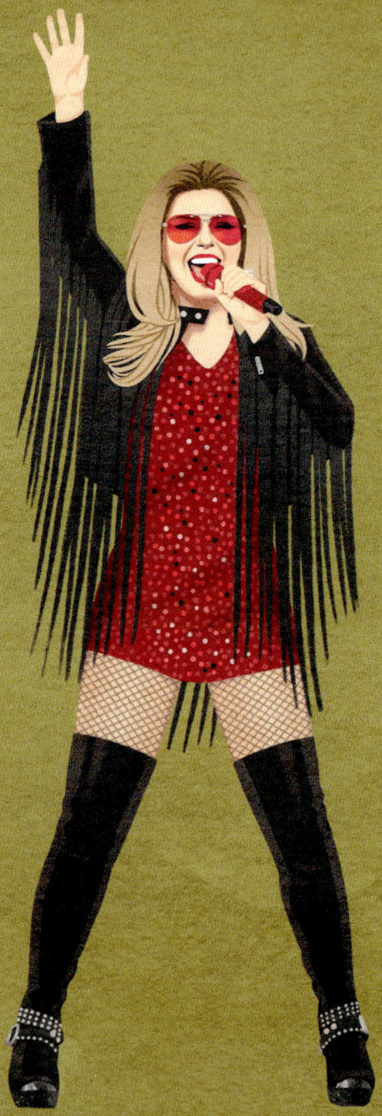

Shania to make a similar post about Dolly Parton) was a sweet acknowledgment of Shania's role in creating a template that has served so many crossover artists who have come up after her.

In January 2022 Shania congratulated Taylor for breaking her previously held record for the female artist with the most weeks on top of the *Billboard* Country Chart. For anyone keeping score, Shania still holds the record for top-selling album by any female artist. Ever. Not that there's any hint of a rivalry: In 2023 Taylor wore a T-shirt with Shania's face and promotional art for "Any Man of Mine," which millions of Swifties took as a message to her then-newish beau Travis Kelce. Maybe so, but Taylor's fashion choice was also a fairly obvious hat-tip to Shania herself. It's impossible to take in the gloriously over-the-top pageantry of Taylor's Eras tour and not think of Shania's sequined and pyrotechnics-laced legacy. Shania has said that she loves her newfound role as "Auntie" to the next gen of performers.

## BEYONCÉ

It's easy to speculate that Beyoncé's transition into country music in 2024 might have been at least partly influenced by the work of the OG pop country poster girl—but we don't have to. Shania shared that shortly after the release of *Cowboy Carter* she received a flower arrangement from a certain Queen of the Bey Hive, saying, "Thank you for the inspiration. I listened to your music all through the making of *Cowboy Carter*."

## HARRY STYLES

It was an intergenerational meeting of icons (never mind a world record for sequin-wearing) in 2022 when Shania made a surprise appearance at Harry Styles's Coachella set. The pair dueted to the chorus of "Man! I Feel Like a Woman!" and, of course, Shania's artistry in the area of gender-bending fashion is easy to find in many of Styles's most famous hooks and lewks. Many have compared the former boy bander to Mick Jagger and David Bowie, but Harry himself had a different answer: "I think in music and fashion my biggest influence has been Shania Twain," he revealed in a 2018 interview. Shania has said that she would love to record with him and even has a song in mind.

## POST MALONE

In a 2019 interview with Jimmy Fallon, the first man of facial ink was asked about what kind of crazy antics he got up to backstage: "It's not really madness, it's a lot of Shania Twain," was his answer. (That and beer pong.) Apparently, Posty has stanned the Queen of Country Pop for a few decades—he used to sing "Man! I Feel Like a Woman!" on the drive to school with his mom. His familiarity with the hit was on full display at the 2019 AMAs, when Shania performed live and Post performed an impassioned lip sync from the front row that later made the rounds on social media. The fandom runs both ways: That same night Twain opened her set with a rendition of Malone's mega-hit "Rock Star."

## ORVILLE PECK

Canada's mask-wearing ranger started writing a duet with Shania Twain mostly as a pipe dream, never imagining that the artist he had worshipped since childhood (his fave ST track is "Forever and For Always") would actually be up for a collab. "I think my brain exploded that day," Peck says of getting the call and eventually making his way to Shania's Vegas ranch to record their duet in the last days before the Covid lockdowns in March 2020. In the video for "Legends Never Die," he sports his signature facial fringe while Shania tips her (bedazzled) Stetson to Peck by adorning her leopard bodysuit with tassels. A critical darling, Peck has faced a lot of backlash for being an openly gay artist on the country scene. Shania has pointed to his success as a "sign that our society is slowly getting there."

## DRAKE

Long before he was the Six God or the Champagne Papi, Drake was a rising star, hosting the Junos (Canada's version of the Grammys) in 2011, and expressing his love for Shania: "Damn, I'd love to make her feel like a woman," he quipped in his opening song. Five years later Twain attended the rapper's show in Nashville, where he professed his love and admiration yet again: "I grew up a fan. I just want to say that, like, Shania Twain came to my show tonight, you know what I'm saying, Nashville? So this next set, right here, I'm doing this for Shania. This is my love set for Shania, right here."

## HALSEY

In the music video for her 2020 hit "You Should Be Sad," the electro-pop princess paid a double homage to her "badass idol" Shania, wearing a vampy look inspired by the "Man! I Feel Like a Woman!" video followed by a hooded leopard bodysuit à la "That Don't Impress Me Much."

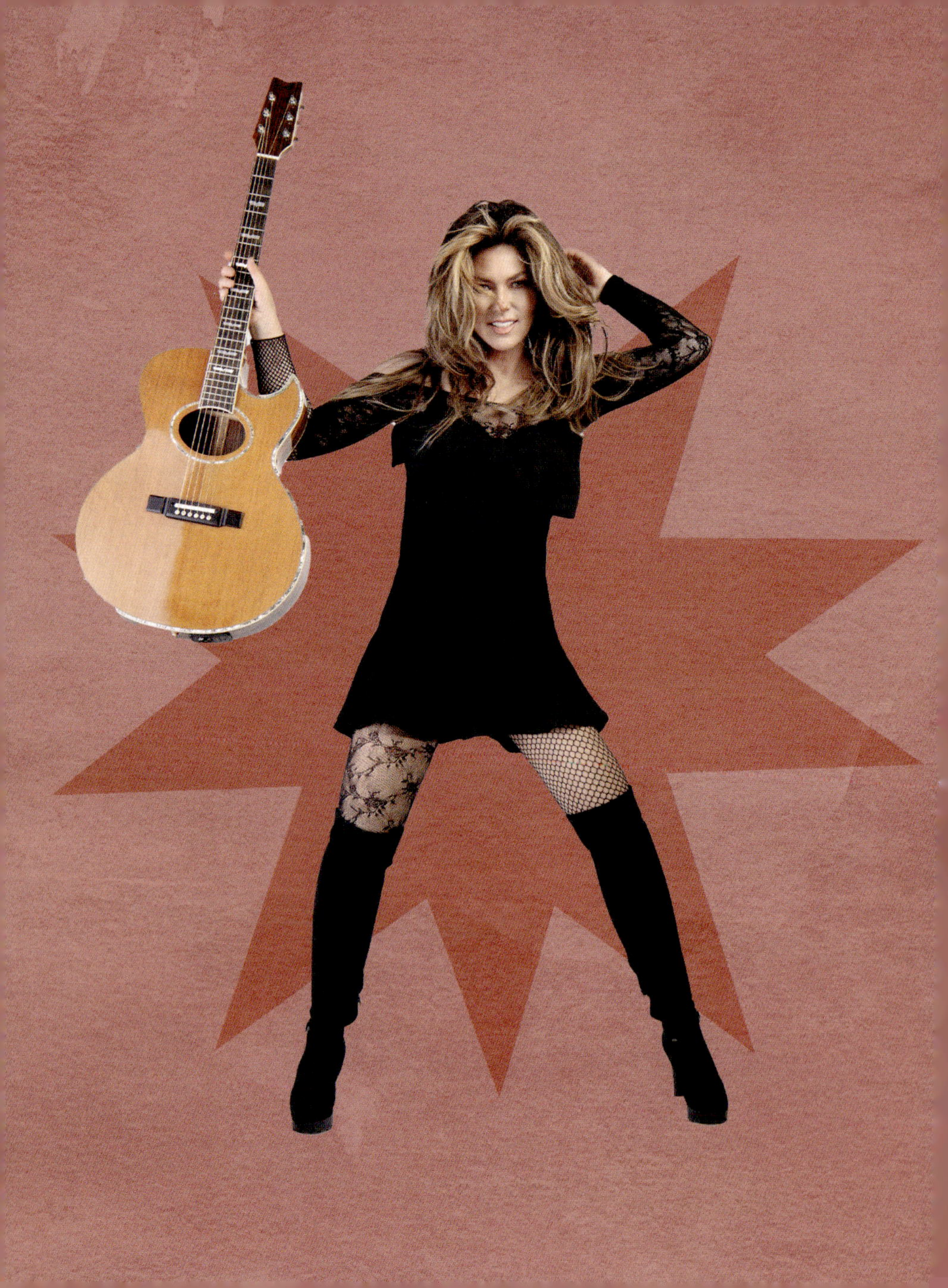

And the influence goes beyond the aesthetic: "The most petty and heartbreaking songs all come from country. I wrote 'YSBS' on my living room floor on my guitar. Lots of time in Nashville, too," Halsey explained on Twitter—unafraid to cross genres thanks to a certain fashionable forebear.

## HAIM

In 2017, the post-genre pop group recorded a pared-down cover of "That Don't Impress Me Much," and the response was so positive that they released it as a single. Clearly the track's title doesn't apply to their feelings about Shania: "I think that's one of the boxes you have to tick if you want to date any of us. You have to be a Shania Twain fan," says Este Haim, one-third of the sister act three-pack.

## AVRIL LAVIGNE

In 1999, a then-sixteen-year-old Avril won a radio contest where the prize was a chance to sing onstage with Shania at her concert in Ottawa. Since then, Twain has been a bit of a fellow Canadian fairy godmother: "Shania Twain redefined what a female artist could be. She showed there were not limits to songwriting, talent, or vision. . . . For every artist who's come after her, she is the inspiration to work harder and keep pushing the boundaries," Lavigne told the audience while presenting her mentor with the ACM Poets Award and then performed Shania's classic "No One Needs to Know," dressed in an outfit that was equal parts Sk8er Girl and pop-country goddess: cowgirl boots and a hooded leopard dress, topped by a studded (and spiked) leather vest.

## KELSEA BALLERINI

The four-time Grammy winner has cited Shania as her most important influence: a pioneer in breaking down barriers to make room for the kind of country pop that Ballerini has built her career on. In 2022 she attended the Academy of Country Music's tribute to Twain wearing a dress that fans recognized instantly: the white, turtlenecked gown, covered in iridescent sequins, that Twain wore to the 1999 Grammys at the peak of her power. The iconic frock wasn't just sitting at the back of a closet; it had to be borrowed from the Grammy Museum, which Ballerini thanked in an Instagram post, writing: "if your hero is shania twain, meet your hero. you may become friends and she may even let you wear THE dress.❤"

## KATY PERRY

Man, Katy Perry feels like a fangirl. The *American Idol* judge performed a few lines from Shania's classic on a 2022 episode. Shania returned the compliment, attending Perry's Vegas residency show, called *Play*, where the pair posed on the suitably pink carpet. "Let's go, girls!" cried Perry in a video that later went viral on TikTok. So much of Perry's career—the amped-up theatrics, the over-the-top outfits, the flirty approach to female empowerment, and forever pushing boundaries—is cut from the cloth of her pop-embracing predecessor.

And a few older icons, too . . .

## ELTON JOHN

Shania grew up singing along to classics like "Goodbye Yellow Brick Road." Back when she cowrote the romantic juggernaut "From This Moment On," her first choice for the male part was Elton John. That didn't work out, maybe because he was more of a "Still the One" fan. The first time Shania met her idol in person was outside of a recording studio, where he walked by her, offering an impromptu rendition of the song's chorus. In 1999 he joined Shania onstage for an epic duet that would later appear on a remastered deluxe edition of *Come On Over*. The pair also performed John's classic "Something

About the Way You Look Tonight." And in this performance, for once, Shania wasn't the one in head-to-toe sequins.

## PRINCE

In 2008 Shania got a phone call from rock royalty. She was in the midst of her split from Mutt Lange at the time, and Prince suggested that they get together to collaborate on the next *Rumours* (the iconic 1977 Fleetwood Mac album that was inspired by romantic breakups within the band). Twain turned the project down, feeling overwhelmed and unworthy at the time, and also struggling with her voice. Twain, who was a major fan, hoped that maybe there would be time for a collaboration in the future, but that door closed with Prince's tragic death in 2016.

CHAPTER SEVEN

# Because Her Fans Are Full-On

"

Don't be stupid. You know I love you.

"

CHAPTER SEVEN

If you've seen Shania live, you know that paying tribute to her devoted fans is a regular feature of her stage act. When she's not pulling them up onstage, she's wearing fan-made fashion creations and (at least once) fawning over their Shania-inspired leg tattoos. Here is a collection of recollections from particularly devoted enthusiasts.

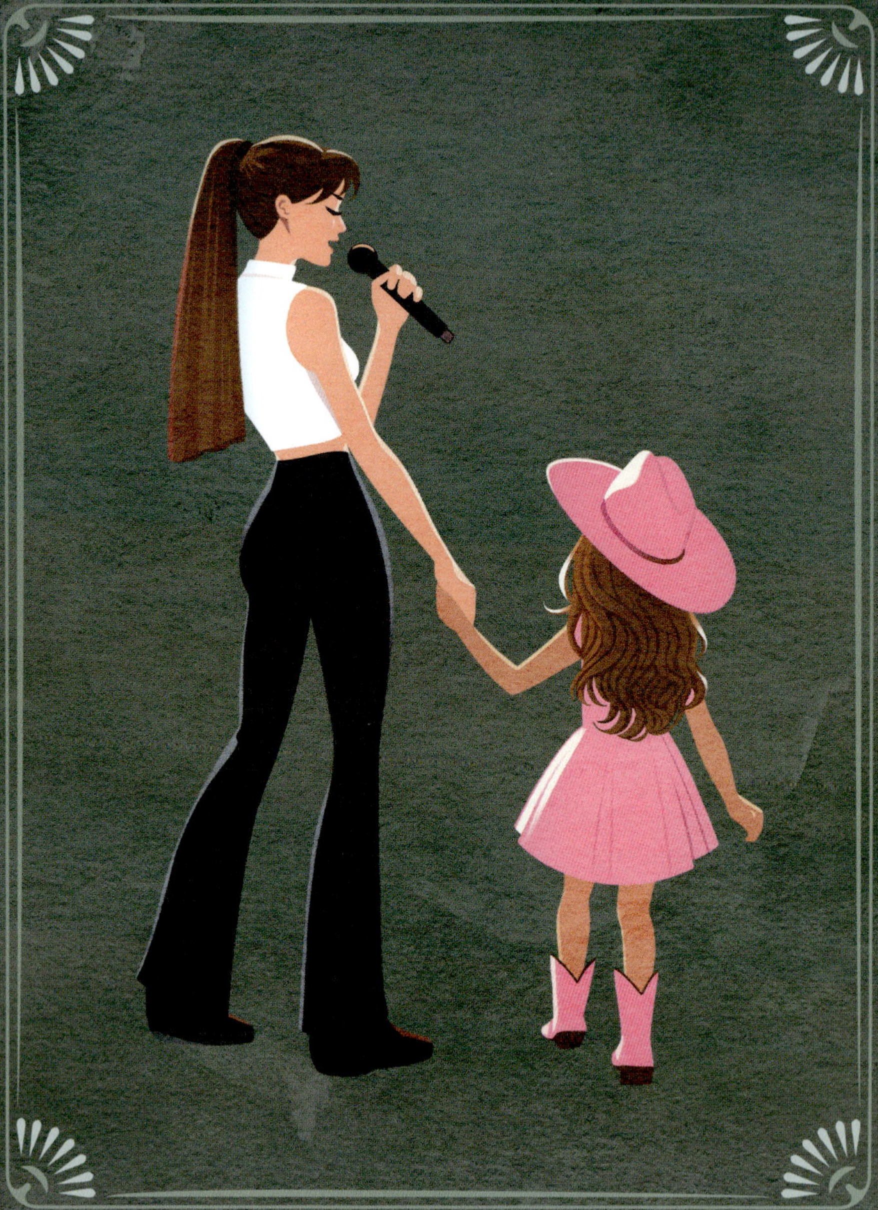

## THE GIDDY-UP GRANDPA

Eighty-one-year-old Ken Northall from Lancashire, England, has spent years seeing Shania perform around the world, and in 2024, Shania returned the favor, performing at the Lytham Festival in Ken's hometown and bringing him up onstage for a version of "That Don't Impress Me Much" that swapped Brad Pitt's name for "Ken."

## HERE COMES THE SUPERFAN

"You're Still the One" has been a popular wedding song for a quarter century now, but Yorkshire, England, bride Sophie Hammill took it one step further by belting out the ode to eternal amour while walking down the aisle. The performance was a surprise to the guests, as well as the groom, who teared up at the surprise serenade.

## CONGRATULATIONS, IT'S A . . . SHANIA FAN

What's even more exciting than learning the sex of your unborn baby? Getting the news from your favorite superstar—live onstage. That's what happened to Hayleigh Gregory, an expectant mom from Newfoundland, Canada, who attended Shania's Toronto concert holding up a sign that read: "Shania, will you do my gender reveal?" Cue the Queen of Creating a Moment ushering her up onstage and performing a personalized rendition of "From This Moment . . . there'll be a girl."

## THE DIVA ON DIVA

Shania is the reason that Daniela Agostino became a singer. At eight years old, she attended the Up! tour with her parents in Toronto and got pulled onstage to join in a rendition of "I'm Gonna Getcha Good." The life-altering experience inspired her to enroll in singing lessons and eventually to study opera. When Shania returned to Toronto on the Queen of Me tour, she remembered her old friend:

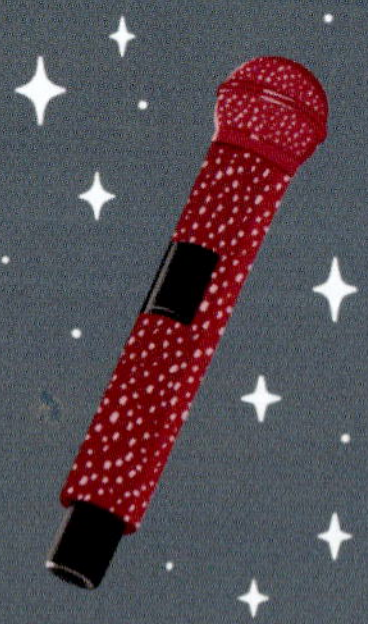

"I know Daniela's here tonight. I think it's time we reunited," she told the packed stadium before pulling Agostino onstage—this time she sang an operatic version of "From This Moment On" and blew her idol away.

## THE DEVOTED DOPPELGÄNGER

Matt Breland has been to more than twenty Shania Twain concerts and owns almost as many of her signature looks. The meteorologist from Louisville joined his idol onstage not once, not twice, but three times during the Queen of Me tour, each time sporting his spin on one of her signature looks (two leopard costumes and the bright yellow Lycra mock-tee from the Up! tour).

## THE BROTHER ACT

Dave and Dan Jones are members of the Ojibwa Indigenous tribe in Canada—the same tribe that Shania belongs to through her Indigenous stepfather. Together they have attended more than seventy of her shows and been invited up onstage (twice!). Dan, who was dressed in the full-on "Man! I Feel Like a Woman!" outfit when he joined his hero onstage in Toronto, has said that growing up on a reservation, it was Shania who inspired him to embrace his individuality.

### THE PINK LADY

Before attending the Queen of Me concert in Manchester, fashion designer Ewan Job posted a photo of the dress he created "for Shania." "It's yours if you want it," he wrote on Instagram, along with a photo of the hot-pink frock. And turns out she did. Through her manager, Shania got in touch with Job's Primaewan label and not long after that she was onstage in the outfit. ("I hope you don't mind if I Shania-fied it," she quipped of her tweak that turned the sleeves into thigh-high boots.)

### THE PUCK PRINCESS

Maple Leafs forward Mitch Marner is a big deal in Canada, but at the Toronto stop on the

2023 Queen of Me tour he surprised his then-bride-to-be (now wife) Stephanie LaChance with an even bigger national treasure. Shania read his message from the stage, "My fiancée is your number-one fan. When she was young, she used to make up dances to all your songs," before inviting the couple to join her onstage.

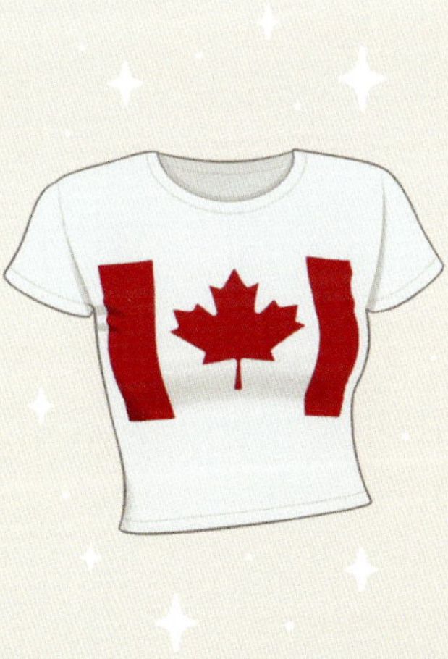

## THE GUY WITH THE THIGH TATTOO

We never got his name, but we'll never forget his upper leg region. A fan at the Saskatoon stop of the Queen of Me tour managed to catch his idol's attention with a tattooed tribute to her hit "Whose Bed Have Your Boots Been Under?" on his upper thigh. "There's a first time for everything," Shania joked as she brought him onstage to sign above the ink—in permanent marker.

## THE MOTHER/DAUGHTER MOMENT

Adalynn Oborowsky was holding a sign that read My first concert when Shania spotted her in the crowd and decided to make the special event even more memorable. The five-year-old, who was at the concert to celebrate Mother's Day with her mega-fan mama Alesha, sang along to "Man! I Feel Like a Woman!" and went home with a guitar pick, a drumstick, and a "What's your first concert?" story for the ages.

## THE COW CLUB

Members of Mississippi State University's Dairy Science Club created a remix and accompanying video to one of Shania's biggest hits. "Any Cow of Mine" features reworked, bovine-appropriate lyrics like: "Any cow of mine better disagree when I say another farmer's working harder than me."

## THE FELLOW QUEEN

As a Shania-loving drag queen, Samantha Stone was used to performing *as* her idol, but not performing *with* her. That changed in 2023, when Stone (dressed in head-to-toe leopard) was invited to come onstage during the Queen of Me tour's stop in Kingston, Ontario. "Okay, so you're Samantha Stone," Shania sang during a duet of "That Don't Impress Me Much."

CHAPTER EIGHT

# Because She's Got More Life Lessons Than Leopard Print (and She's Got a Lot of Leopard Print)

“Ain’t nothin’ better. We beat the odds together.”

# CHAPTER EIGHT

Anyone currently on the hunt for a life mantra could do a lot worse than WWSD? (that's What would Shania do?). Over six decades, she has seen highs and lows and collected a whole lot of hard-won wisdom, and you don't have to be a globally recognized icon to live by her essential mantras. Enjoy a few more reasons to love Shania, along with a dose of inspiration.

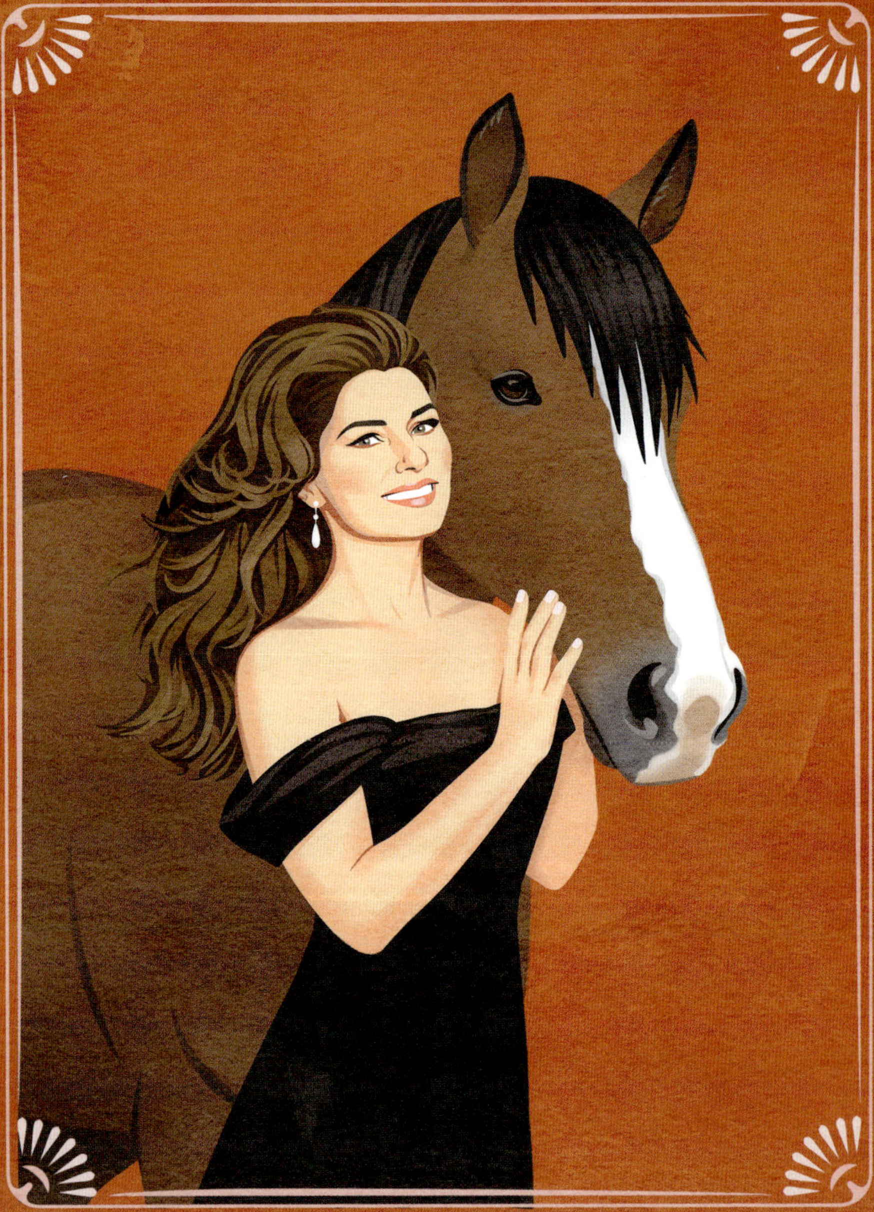

## HORSE-HUGGING IS A GREAT SELF-CARE HACK.

Horses have always been a source of comfort for Shania, not just riding them, but turning to them to manage her anxiety, as she explained during a 2023 interview with Drew Barrymore. Having trouble sleeping or just staying calm in the chaos? Consider cozying up to the closest equine, which is what Shania will sometimes do in the middle of the night, heading down to the barn, entering a stall, and hugging whichever horse is available.

## MUSIC IS THE ONLY UPPER YOU NEED.

As a teenager and twenty-something, Shania spent time with friends who got wasted rocking out to the hits of the moment. But, for her, a chemical boost was never necessary: "You guys want to put a few things on your tongue, do acid, you just go ahead," she once told friends before seeing Pink Floyd live. Meanwhile, she

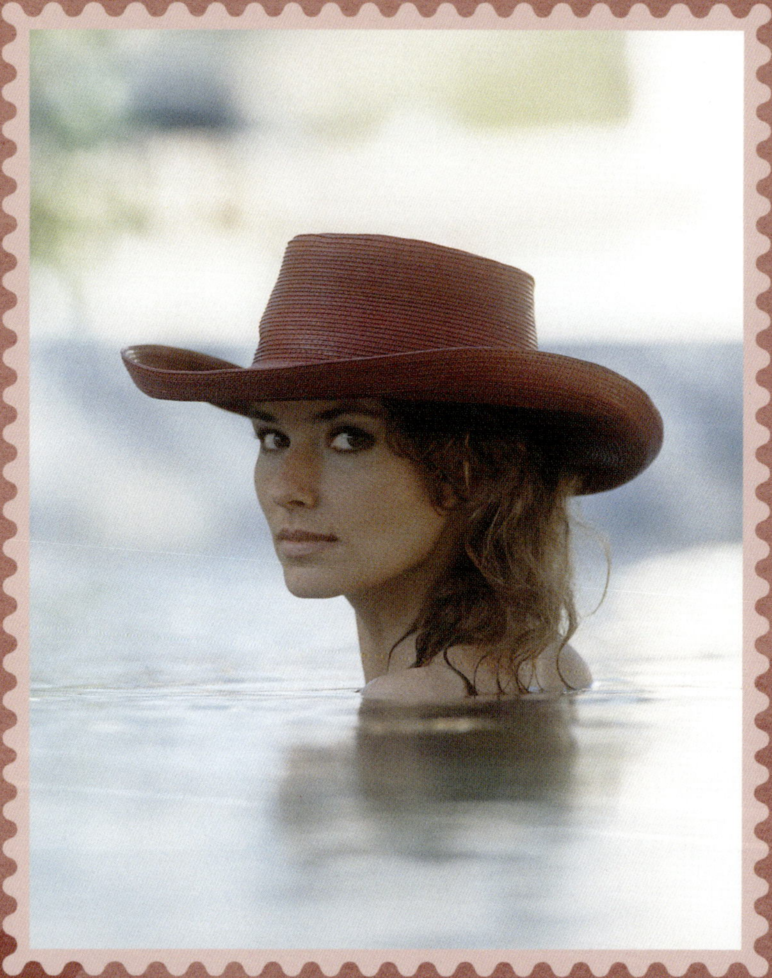

would get asked whether she was "high on something," based on her enthusiastic dance moves. Nope—not unless you count a killer guitar solo.

### YOU'RE RESPONSIBLE FOR YOUR OWN GOOD VIBES.

So much iconic music has come to us via songwriters who lean into their personal tragedy, which is a perfectly legitimate artistic instinct, but Shania has always seen positivity as her secret weapon. Her 2023 album, *The Queen of Me*, started as an exercise in escaping the emotional funk that came following the pandemic, a life-threatening bout of Covid, and renewed vocal distress because of it. Rather than wallow, she told herself that she had the power to put some giddy in her up (and then she wrote a song celebrating that exact message). "I started writing lyrics that made me smile and laugh, and melodies and rhythms that made me want to dance. And it worked. It was this fabulous

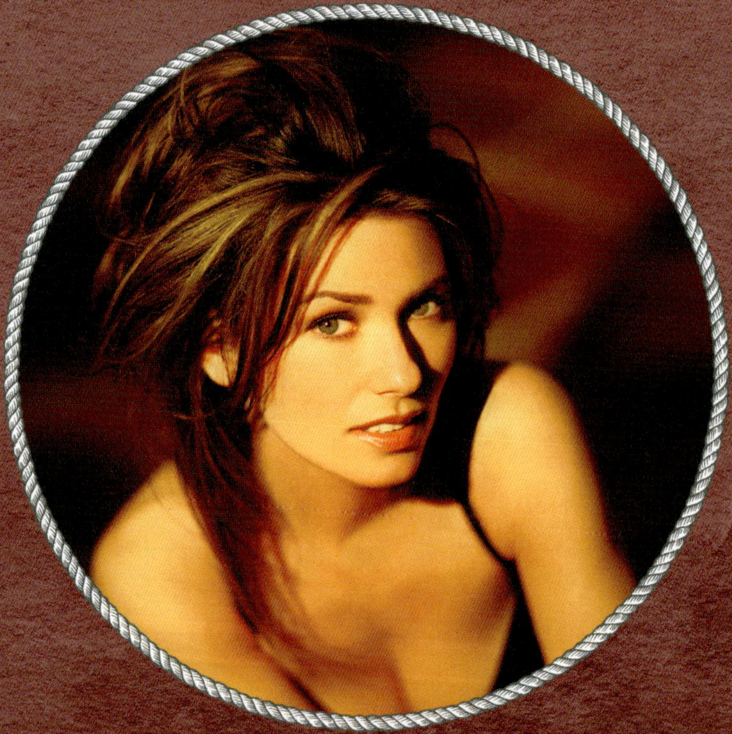

therapy that ended up becoming my happy album." Almost all of Shania's music is upbeat, not because she doesn't have dark times to draw on (she's got plenty), but because she believes in the power of positive vibing.

## THE PAST IS EXACTLY THAT.

After her recovery from dysphonia and open-throat surgery in 2018, much of the music world was preoccupied with whether that world-famous set of pipes would ever be the same. Which is a huge amount of pressure and also beside the point. Change is a part of life, and getting caught up in what *was* (no matter how pitch-perfect) is a good way to miss out on what *is*. Post–Lyme disease, dysphonia, and two open-throat surgeries, Shania's new voice is "raspy, airy, sexy" (her words)—and she's not looking back.

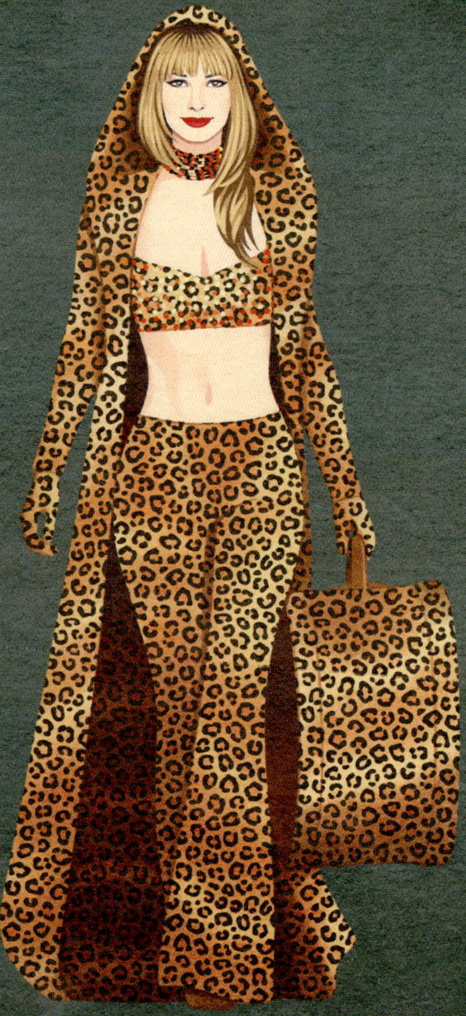

## THE CRITIC THAT COUNTS MOST IS THE ONE IN THE MIRROR.

When she was first getting started, Shania was faced with an endless amount of input from industry folk who felt like they knew what her sound should be like, how she should dress, how much of her belly she should show. A moment of revelation came when she decided the person she should most worry about pleasing wasn't her boosters or her critics, but herself. "Everyone kept telling me I was never going to make it and I realized that if I was going to fail being myself or fail being some fake version of me, I was going to do the former. At least that way I would still have my own respect."

## THERE IS (NO SUCH THING AS) **TOO** MUCH PUNCTUATION!

If there was a world record for exclamation points and parentheses in song titles, it would surely go to Shania (!!!), whose appreciation for punctuation speaks to a broader (and less

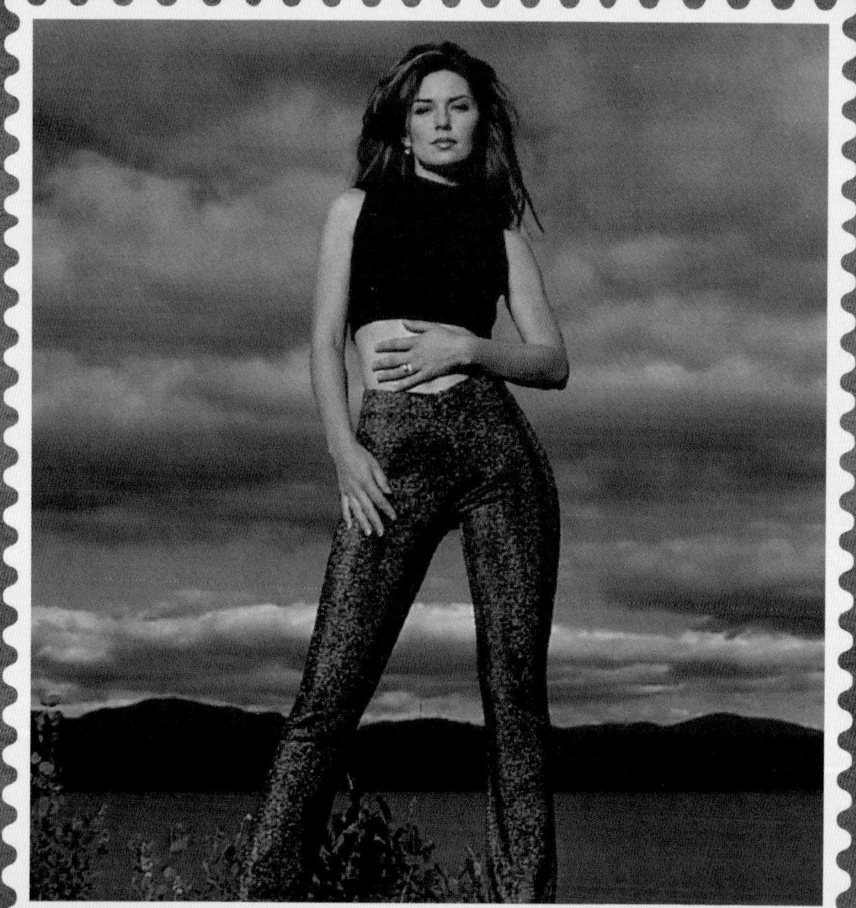

boring) worldview. It's one that embraces public displays of enthusiasm over apathy and eye rolls. When a moment is worth celebrating, go ahead (and celebrate!!!).

## BASIC DOESN'T HAVE TO MEAN BORING.

At least not in Shania's closet. "Leopard is my neutral," she once told *Elle* magazine during a wardrobe-focused walk down memory lane where she discussed her decades-long love affair with the iconic animal print. There is the velvet jumpsuit from "That Don't Impress Me Much" (obviously), but for Shania, embracing leopard print means fitting what may seem like a "bold" expression into everyday life. "Leopard belongs everywhere" is her take. And, let's face it, the world doesn't need more taupe. (Meow.)

## IT'S A GOOD IDEA TO KEEP YOUR GRAMMYS WHERE YOU CAN SEE 'EM.

Shania has won more than two hundred awards over the course of her career, including five Grammys. For the longest time she kept them all in a storage room of her house's lower level until her son, Eja, encouraged her to put them on display. "It's not that I don't appreciate the awards," she said on the *LadyGang* podcast in 2020. "I guess it just took his sense of appreciation. He was proud and he wants me to enjoy my accomplishments."

## IT'S OKAY TO PUT DOWN YOUR SWORD.

Shania is all about fighting for what she believes in, but she has also learned that some battles—take aging, for example—are unwinnable and when you focus all your time and energy on things that won't happen, you rob yourself of the chance to work toward the things that might.

## BETRAYAL IS A GOOD TEACHER.

Shania has made no secret of the breakdown she experienced after her first husband stabbed her in the heart by having an affair with his assistant, and her best friend (that assistant) stabbed her in the back by sleeping with her husband. But, with some time to heal, she has learned to see the upside: "Now that you are wise to the game, you have the tools to choose your friends more carefully and protect your inner circle from these predators. Wear your scars like a badge."

## A GOOD BLENDER IS A GODSEND.

Living on the road and following a liquids-only diet on show days means that Shania counts her blender among her best friends. (In case you're wondering, coconut water, apple, and avocado is her go-to smoothie.)

# The Bonus Content

“

I'm keeping you forever and for always.

”

# Quizzes to Test Your Shania Fandom

**To know her is to love her, but just how deep does your Shania devotion run?**

**1. Shania often uses this song to do her vocal warm-ups:**

**A.** "You Oughta Know" by Alanis Morissette
**B.** "Come Over" by Carly Rae Jepsen
**C.** "One Less Lonely Girl" by Justin Bieber
**D.** "I Drove All Night" by Celine Dion

**2. Shania has said that she is very inspired by this fellow crop-top enthusiast and loves to sing along to their albums:**

**A.** Britney Spears
**B.** Christina Aguilera
**C.** Gwen Stefani
**D.** Ricky Martin

**3. A running gag about Shania Twain and "tuna tofu" in the script to this early aughts "existential comedy" led Shania to guest-star:**

**A.** *The Royal Tenenbaums*
**B.** *I Heart Huckabees*
**C.** *He's Just Not That into You*
**D.** *Napoleon Dynamite*

**4. Shania has appeared on all but one of the following reality series:**

**A.** *The Bachelor*
**B.** *Keeping Up with the Kardashians*
**C.** *American Idol*
**D.** *Dancing with the Stars*

**5. In 2021, Shania provided the narration for *For Love*, a Canadian documentary about this important issue:**

**A.** Seal-clubbing
**B.** Indigenous children in foster care
**C.** Indigenous land rights
**D.** Climate change

**6. Which hip-hop star rapped "Shania Twain, notepad, I'm makin' it line dance"?**

**A.** The Weeknd
**B.** Kanye West
**C.** Drake
**D.** Eminem

**7. Shania made her acting debut in 2019 alongside this Oscar-winning actor:**

**A.** Tom Cruise
**B.** Denzel Washington
**C.** Brad Pitt
**D.** John Travolta

**8. The Shania Twain Canadian postage stamp, issued in 2013, features that national treasure in this outfit:**

**A.** Leopard bodysuit
**B.** Top hat and mini-veil
**C.** Black off-the-shoulder top
**D.** Neon-yellow nylon top

**9. During her 2022 People's Choice Awards performance of "That Don't Impress Me Much," Shania swapped out Brad Pitt's name for this fellow Canadian:**

**A.** Ryan Reynolds
**B.** Ryan Gosling
**C.** Drake
**D.** Justin Trudeau

**10. When she performed the halftime show at the 2017 Grey Cup, Shania arrived via this mode of transport:**

**A.** Helicopter
**B.** Horseback
**C.** Hang glider
**D.** Dogsled

**11. In 2022 this celebrity entrepreneur got Shania to play a secret concert for her hairdresser before his wedding:**

**A.** Gwyneth Paltrow
**B.** Chrissy Teigen
**C.** Kim Kardashian
**D.** Kylie Jenner

**12. In 2024 Shania made a cameo appearance in this Netflix series, performing a private concert at the lead character's sixtieth birthday bash:**

**A.** *A Man in Full*
**B.** *Umbrella Academy*
**C.** *Baby Reindeer*
**D.** *The Diplomat*

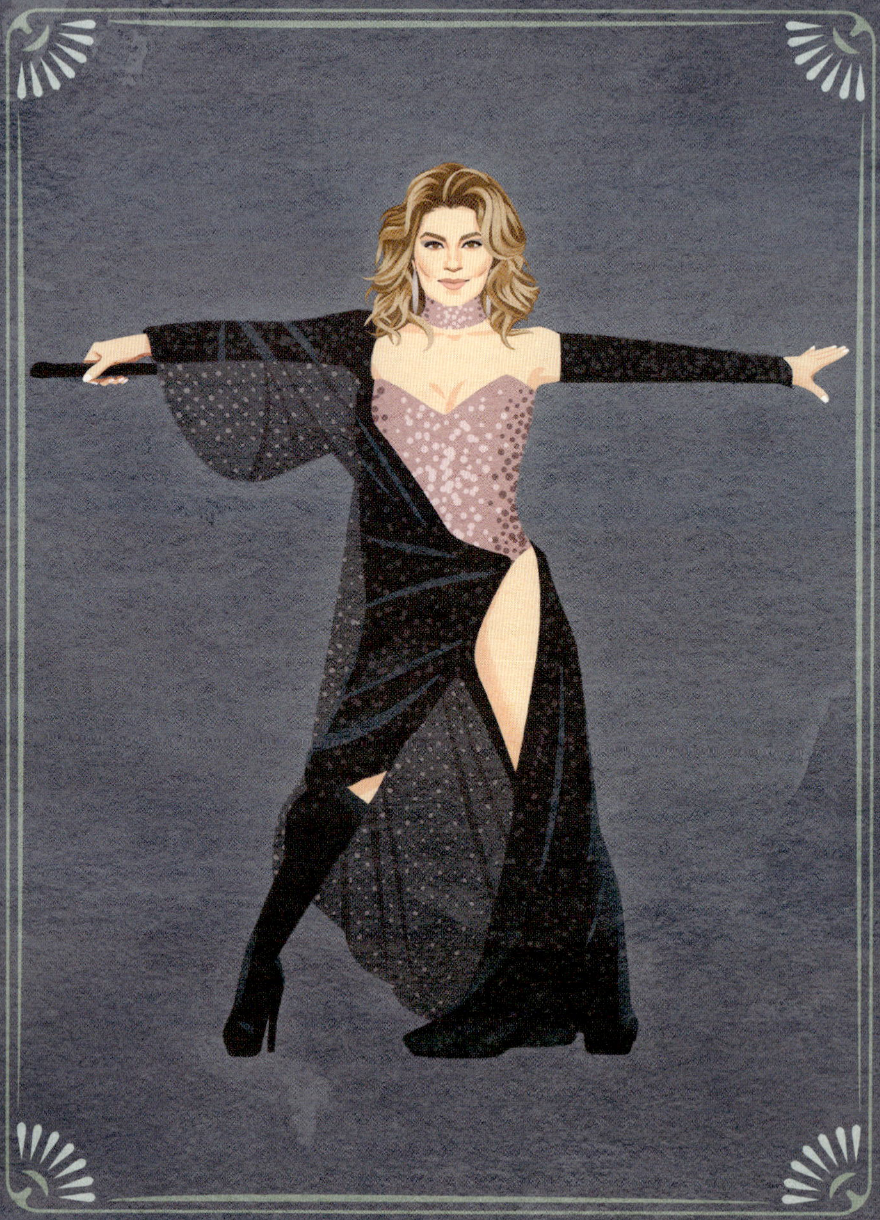

## ANSWERS:

**D, A, B, A, B, C, D, B, A, D, C, A**

## 0–3: CAN ONLY GO UP! FROM HERE

Lucky you—your Shania knowledge is minimal, which means it's time to take a deep dive into her leopard-printed past.

## 4–6: THAT DON'T IMPRESS ME MUCH

And you call yourself a Shania fan? You need to spend a little time brushing up before the next tour.

## 7–9: GIDDY UP!

Clearly you know your stuff, but there is still room for improvement. Time to set up that Shania Google alert.

## 10–12: MAN! YOU FEEL LIKE A MEGA-FAN!

We'd say, "let's go, girls," but clearly you're already there. Congrats on your ultimate fan status!

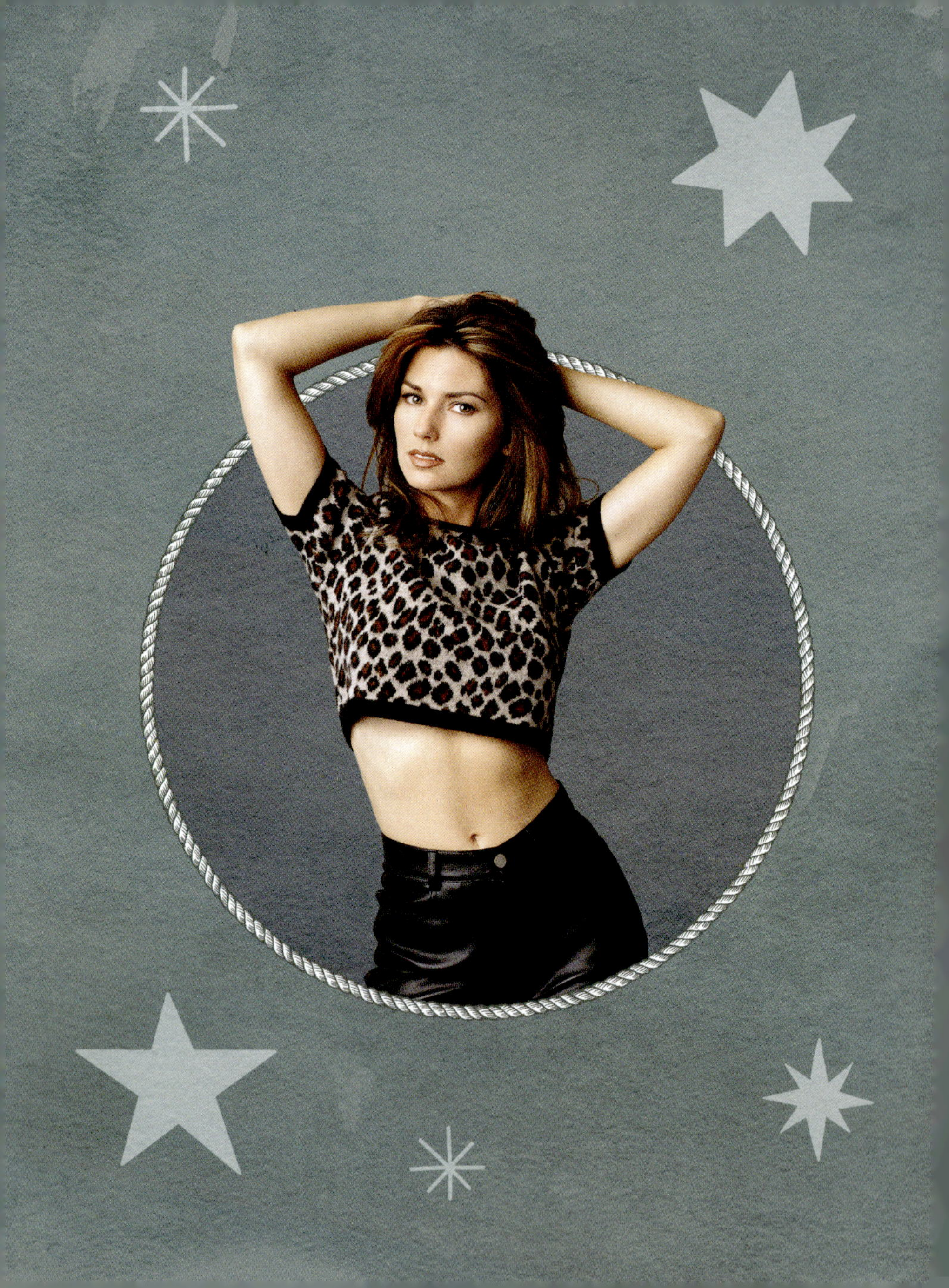

# Which Iconic Shania Look Are You?

Shania serves up iconic fashion moments like In-N-Out serves up burgers, but which one is best representative of your personal vibe?

**1. Your favorite kind of movie:**

**A.** Goofball comedies
**B.** Old Hollywood classics
**C.** Political thrillers
**D.** Hot-and-heavy romances

**2. Your preferred kind of self-care:**

**A.** Being outdoors and ideally on a horse
**B.** Mani/pedi and massage
**C.** Curling up with a book
**D.** Bubble bath for two

**3. Your high school yearbook said you were "Most likely to . . ."**

**A.** Own more animals than Old MacDonald
**B.** Land your dream job and marry your high school sweetheart
**C.** Run for president
**D.** Be a soap opera star

**4. You can't resist a romantic partner who:**

**A.** Chops their own firewood

**B.** Shows up in a stretch limo with long-stemmed roses

**C.** Suggests splitting the bill

**D.** Doesn't leave home without a DO NOT DISTURB sign

**5. The fashion era you identify with most closely is:**

**A.** The 1960s: bell-bottoms and Birkenstocks

**B.** The 1990s: understated body-con

**C.** The 2010s: gender is an outdated concept

**D.** The 1980s: more is more

**6. Concert (other than Shania's) that you wouldn't miss:**

**A.** Taylor Swift

**B.** Beyoncé

**C.** Lady Gaga

**D.** Rihanna

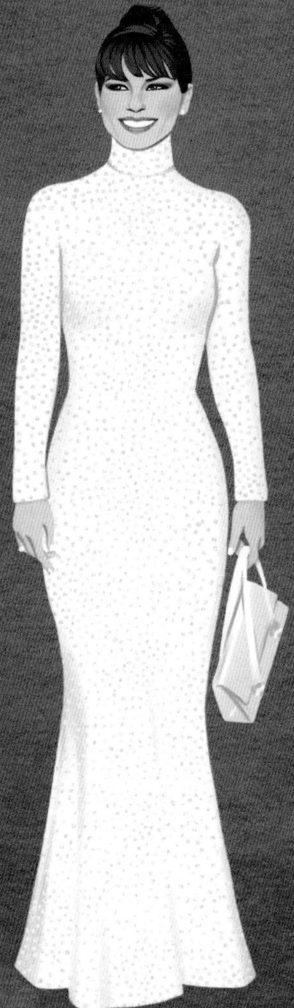

**7. At a job interview you are asked to identify a weakness, and you answer:**

**A.** I tend to stick with what's comfortable

**B.** I'm a perfectionist

**C.** I won't give up the good fight

**D.** Weakness—what weakness?

**8. Must-have accessory:**

**A.** Cowboy hat

**B.** Pearl earrings

**C.** Top hat and tassled riding crop

**D.** Choker

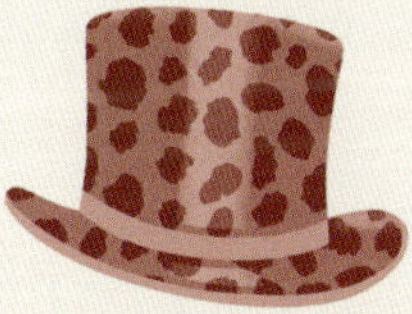

## MOSTLY As

### You're a Blue Jean Baby

See: The denim-on-denim "Canadian tuxedo" that Shania wore in the "Any Man of Mine" video.

Fashion is great as long as it doesn't keep you from doing the things you love. Your runway is the great outdoors and your version of dressing up is the pair of jeans that doesn't have any holes (yet).

## MOSTLY Bs

### You're an Eternal Icon

See: The white gown that Shania wore on the red carpet at the 1999 Grammys.

The classics are classic for a reason. You're confident enough to keep your luxury quiet and the only trends you care to follow are the ones that stand the test of time.

## MOSTLY Cs

### You're a Fashion Statement

See: The sexy, androgynous ringmaster from the "Man! I Feel Like a Woman!" video.

Rules are made to be broken—in style and in life. For you, fashion is a form of self-expression and a way to push important conversations (and eye-catching accessories) into the mainstream.

## MOSTLY Ds

### You're a Flirty Feline

See: The hooded leopard bodysuit from the "That Don't Impress Me Much" video.

You make no apologies for your signature sex appeal, often best expressed in animal print. Confidence is the ultimate aphrodisiac and your closet is full of it—meow.

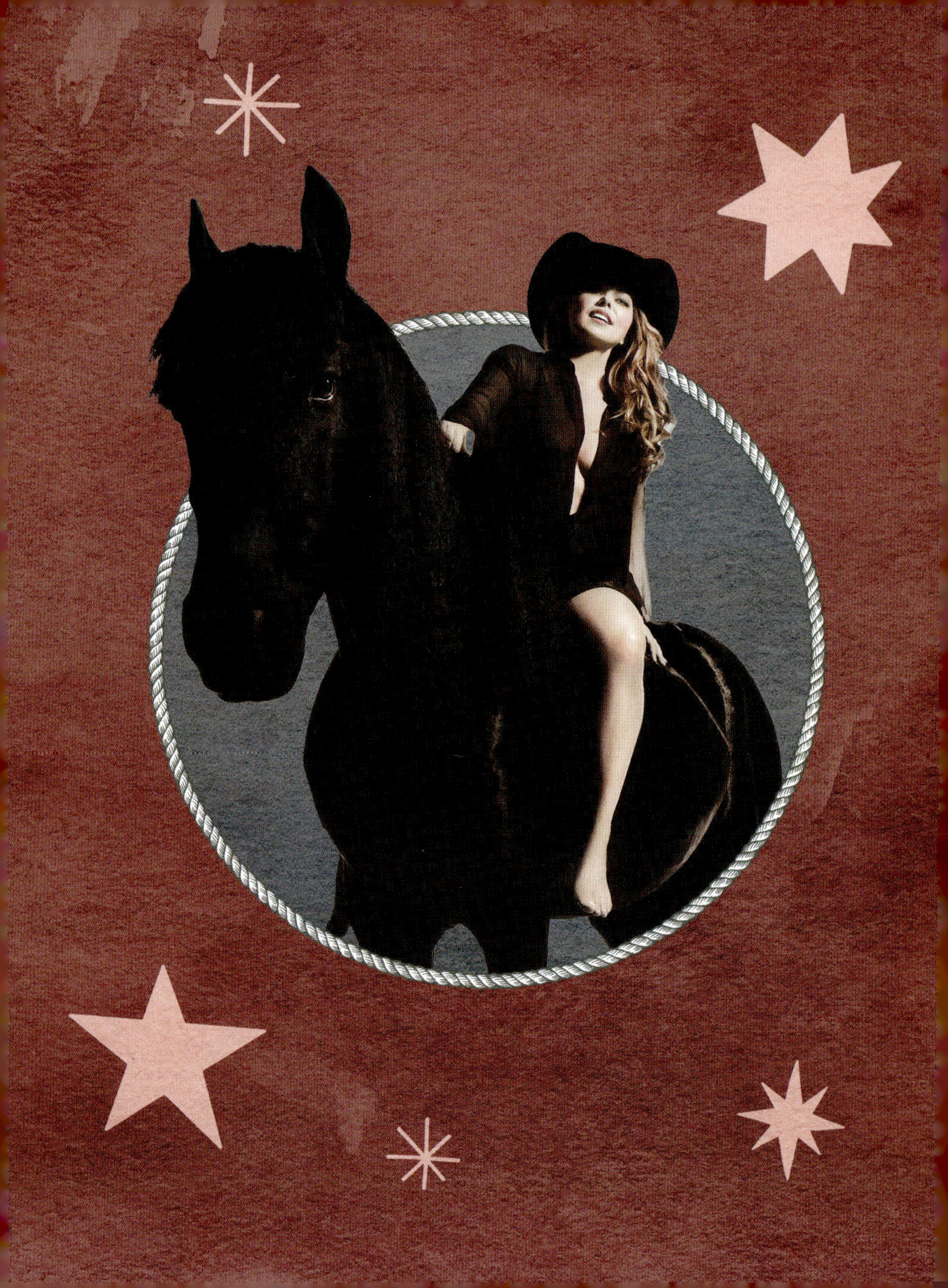

# The Shaniassance

When music historians look back on the origins of the Shaniassance, some may point to the release of *Queen of Me*—the singer's sixth studio album, which came out in 2022, heralding a new era of good vibes and personal empowerment. (Not to mention a new wardrobe and rotation of candy-colored wigs!) Others will land on her iconic Coachella performance opposite Harry Styles that same year as the moment of maximum cultural

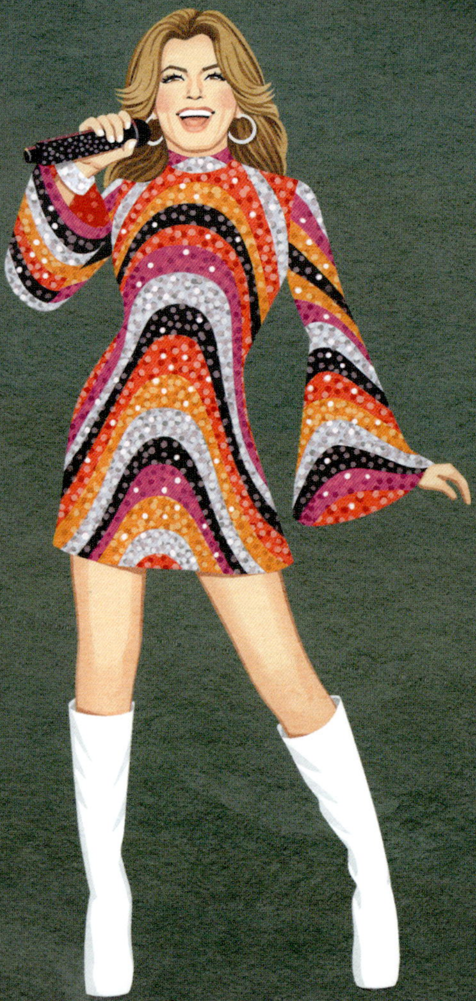

saturation. There is also the Netflix special *Not Just a Girl*, where the largely private public figure brings her fans behind the scenes to reflect on hard-won wisdom and celebrate being the captain of her own destiny.

Many so-called "heritage acts" enjoy renewed popularity years and even decades later. Nostalgia is a gift that keeps on giving (and selling concert tickets), hence massive tours from bands and solo artists whose heyday was on the other side of the turn of new millennium. But unlike so many older acts, Shania's popularity in the 2020s is more than just a blast from the past. Yes, her fans include those of us who came of age during her first wave of success, but just as many weren't even born yet when *Come On Over* was released. These are the crowds catching the Queen of Country Pop at Coachella or Glastonbury or Boots and Hearts or Stagecoach—the Gen Z diehards who are remixing her classics on TikTok and ensuring that her streaming stats are up there with contemporary chart-toppers. According to data from Spotify, the surge in downloads of nineties country is being spurred not by the original audience but by listeners in their twenties and thirties who see country as just pop and can barely imagine a time when that wasn't the case.

Mainstream music charts, once dominated by boy bands and hip-hop, feature a huge class of country talent. It's the superstars who have their roots in Nashville (think Taylor Swift) and the massive names from other genres (Beyoncé, Post Malone) who have unleashed their inner cowboys and cowgirls because genre is an outdated concept that has nothing to do with what audiences want to hear. Huh—it's almost like Shania knew what she was talking about all those years ago when she took in the various rules and conventions governing country music and decided that they just didn't impress her much. Three decades later and she's certainly earned the right to relax—to lie back in a leopard-print La-Z-Boy and survey the modern musicscape that wouldn't be what it is today without her. Except that—sigh—the more things change . . .

In the 2020s, women in country continue to fight for airtime as bro country enjoys a resurgence alongside regressive political movements. This is even more true for LGBTQ+ country artists and country artists of color, which is why representatives from these communities were invited to perform on the Queen of Me tour. Classic Shania—fighting back against a toxic reality with good vibes and even better music. (Maybe when she's done with entertainment she should consider running for Queen of the World.)

But she's not done—nowhere near it. Since releasing *Queen of Me*, she has been all over the place—on stages, red carpets, and social media, serving up fashion and fodder for her fans and sass for her critics (some of whom still don't seem to have gotten the message about women wearing crop tops). Her belly-baring outfit at the 2023 CMT Awards may have been "controversial" to a certain strain of pearl-clutching killjoys, but for Shania the look was about looking fierce and having fun and offering a bit of an IYKYK wink to the ones who have been with her all along. The first award she ever received was a Rising Star Award from CMT back in 1993, and thirty years later she was back on the same stage, being honored for her efforts to promote inclusivity.

Another full-circle moment came in 2023 when Mattel released a Shania Twain Barbie—one of several special editions celebrating the sixty-year anniversary of International Women's Day. Having your own Barbie is a big deal for anyone but maybe that much more meaningful for the girl from small-town Ontario who used to play with blades of grass because dolls were too expensive. Shania Barbie is dressed in a miniaturized version of the

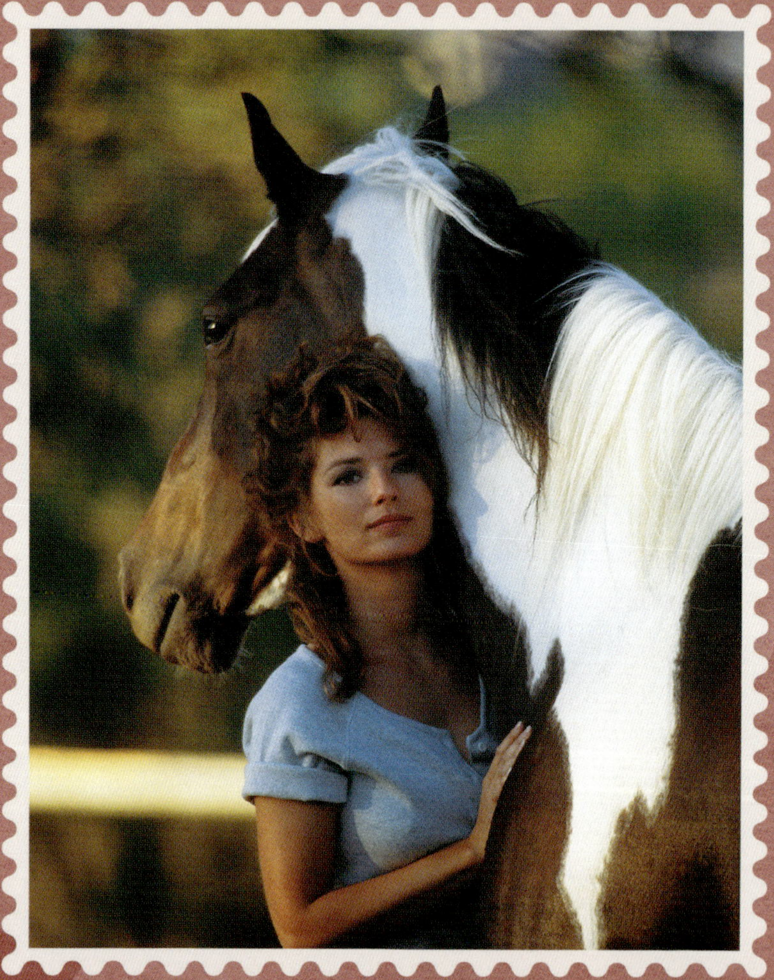

"Man! I Feel Like a Woman!" wardrobe: a teeny-tiny top hat and cape. Thirty years ago that song inspired a generation of fans to fight for what's right and to have a little fun while they're at it. And if there's one final reason to heart Shania, it's because she's all about practicing what you preach.

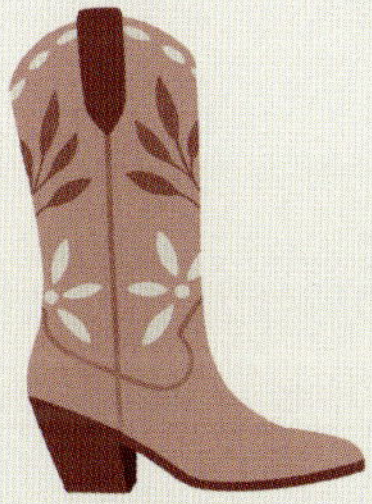

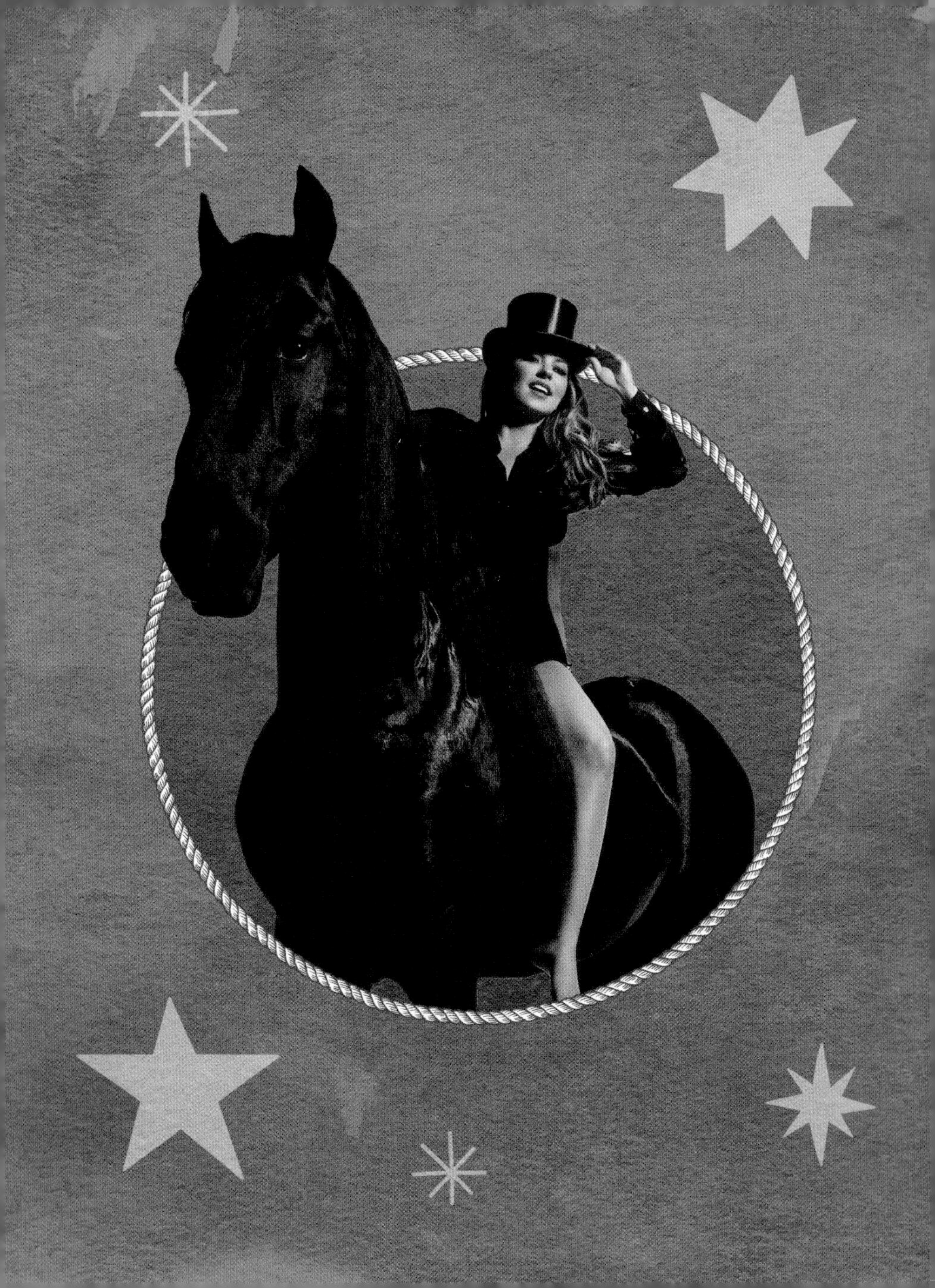

# Exclusive Q&A with Shania

What's better than writing a book about Shania Twain? Actually getting a chance to talk to her. Somewhere in between her festival gigs and awards show appearances, the Queen of Country Pop made time for an *exclusive* interview and now we have to add "Because she took a call while helping her friend wrangle cattle" to our list of reasons to love her.

**CS:** When you began your career there were very strict rules about genre and picking a lane between pop and country music. Today country is pop. Does that give you a sense of satisfaction? Like, hey, I did that.

**ST:** I don't know why it took so long! The country music that I grew up with in Northern Ontario in Canada was very diverse. I would listen to Charlie Pride, the Carpenters, Gordon Lightfoot, Joni Mitchell—a lot of folk was mixed into that style of old-time country. You had someone like Dolly Parton crossing into pop. Kenny Rogers came out of rock before he went country and so that sense of blending was just normal to me. And then I got to Nashville and it was like, no, you can't do that. I started crossing genres in the nineties and then there was this long gap, so it's definitely nice to see music coming around to that again. I don't think fans care about genre—they just want good music that speaks to them, whether it's bluegrass or rock or soul. Country music has always been about storytelling. It takes more than a banjo to make a great country song.

**CS:** You mentioned Dolly, who was an idol to you just like you are an idol to so many of today's performers . . .

**ST:** No one did it better than Dolly Parton. She's a hillbilly at heart, but just as much as she can strum on her banjo she can write pop songs that travel all over the world. She loves the glitz and glamour that she certainly didn't see growing up in the hills of Tennessee.

**CS:** And I'm guessing your sense of pageantry and fashion didn't come from the Canadian backwoods—

**ST:** I wasn't raised with any of that and even today my everyday life is very basic and simple. Like today, I'm on a horse, so I'm not wearing any sequins. But the performance side of things, particularly video and photography, was a place for me to explore and expand my love of art direction and fashion. It gave me a platform to experiment from and I just loved it and it felt so natural for me to play with silhouettes, to know how to use lighting. I didn't have an opportunity to express these skills until my first video, but, when I did, it was like I had always known. Like a sixth sense.

**CS:** Not to switch topics, but you're on a horse today, like right now while we're talking?

**ST:** I hadn't planned to be, but the cattle drive got delayed, so here I am. That's okay with me. I'm perfectly happy chatting in the saddle.

**CS:** Is this one of your own horses?

**ST:** No, no. Today I'm riding a porter horse in Alberta, helping my friends move their cattle from one field to another, so we've just finished crossing a river. It's a real freedom. It's funny, the first time I did this—herd cattle—was during the shoot for the "Any Man of Mine" video. From then on, I was like, "horses have to be in my life forever," so it was a personal life change that came from making a music video.

**CS:** I love that. Any other videos stand out?

**ST:** I think the most challenging was the shoot for "Party for Two." That was shot with two different artists—Mark McGrath sang the pop version and Billy Currington sang the country. It was forty-eight hours of nonstop, definitely a test of my endurance. The video for "Ka-Ching" is my favorite styling—everything was done by hand and then as far as overall aesthetic, shots, angles, I would say "That Don't Impress Me Much."

**CS:** Of your many leopard outfits, that has to be the most iconic.

**ST:** That was a design I collaborated with Marc Bouwer on from head to toe and it just turned out so beautifully. I still have the original at home. So many good memories. I actually camped overnight in the desert the night before. It was quite remote so there were no hotels. Everyone else had to drive an hour and a half, so I was like, I'm not doing that.

**CS:** I guess those Canadian camping skills come in handy?

**ST:** That's it.

**CS:** You are obviously aware of the current Shaniassance. What is it about your music that is still resonating with new fans all these years later?

**ST:** I think when records are well made and easy to listen to, they hold up. A lot of kids who are listening now may have gotten a hint of it when they were toddlers, so they were drawn in by the nostalgia, but then they took ownership of it by themselves. One thing about country music is that the stories speak to the masses, no matter the time or the type of life you come from. It's not the kind of lingo or terminology that feels dated after a certain amount of time.

**CS:** Is there any particular Shania anthem you are glad to see getting the redux treatment?

**ST:** "Any Man of Mine" ticks all the boxes in terms of nostalgia. It's about self-empowerment, taking ownership of your own happiness. That's one that gets a lot of love from any age, any genre.

**CS:** Speaking of empowerment anthems, women in country are still fighting to be heard, much as you were fighting twenty-five years ago. Is that surprising? Frustrating?

**ST:** I think what happens is that the industry—the record companies, executives, publishing houses, etc.—feel that men are more relatable, so they gear the songwriters to write songs from the perspective of men and then the best songs go to the male artists and you get this problematic cycle. It's a songwriting gap.

**CS:** You experienced that gap when you were getting started in Nashville. Is it fair to say that your solution was to write your own hits?

**ST:** That's it. At the time, a lot of the executives were saying, you get can't everyone. Either you get the men and because of that the women will hate you or it's vice versa. I just didn't believe that was true, in my gut. I was very conscious about writing songs with conversational lyrics. I spoke to the men with a sense of humor instead of at them. And the modern woman I could speak to because I really related. There's a lot of pressure on women to do everything and to do it well. I wrote songs that let women know that I understood them. I became their advocate and their cheerleader just by sharing my own experience. Being my authentic self was important to me from the start. So many people were telling me I was going to fail, so my thought was, if I do this and I'm not being my authentic self, I'm going to hate it whether I succeed or not, so I might as well stick to my guns.

**CS:** **Twenty-five years ago you said the best thing about being a woman is the prerogative to have a little fun. Is that still the case?**

**ST:** Absolutely! More now than ever. If you're going to enjoy your life, you have to let go of a lot of your fears. I'm more fearless than I have ever been and I'm having a lot more fun because of it.